If you are thinking of working as a waiter or waitress while in school, between "real" jobs, or to earn some extra income; or if you are currently working as a Server and feel you are not getting everything you deserve, this book is for you.

Recent surveys show customers spend over $175 billion dollars a year in America's restaurants. If that money was divided evenly among all 50 states, restaurants in each state would take in $3.5 billion dollars. Tips for the waiters and waitresses in each state would total five and a quarter million dollars! The information in this book will help you get your share.

During my 15 years in and around the restaurant business, I spent hundreds of hours collecting the most effective money-making and aggravation-saving strategies from the best waiters and waitresses in the country. These techniques have been used successfully in all types of restaurants; from coast to coast, and in America's heartland. And they will work for you!

Even though each technique in this book is some server's tried and true favorite, not every one of them will fit your personality. And yes, some of these strategies will be more effective for women, some for men; some if you are older, and some if you are younger. But virtually every strategy and technique can be adapted to fit the restaurant environment you are working in and your personality.

You will get the most out of this book if you read it through once and then go back and read 3 - 4 pages before you go to work each day. Try it all out and keep what works best for you. I guarantee you will be a smarter sever. And that's our goal because smarter servers give better service and earn great tips!

Now let's get started.

For additional copies of this book,
please contact:

BookMasters Inc.   800 - 247 - 6553

www.BookMasters.com/GreatTips

To arrange a training seminar for your staff
or school group, please contact the author directly.
e-mail: cyrelson@mkl.com

Printed in the United States of America
by BookMasters Inc.

Copyright 1995
First Printing 1996
Second Printing 1999

Acknowledgments

Although I learned a lot during my years as a
server, most of the material in this book is based on
conversations with hundreds of waiters and waitresses who
practiced on thousands of customers. Where possible, I
have tried to give direct credit. To all those I have failed to
recognize by name, I offer my sincerest thanks.

This book is dedicated to Barry Chilkotowsky for
taking a novice under his wing many years ago; to Rachel
Catling, a great diner waitress, who found time between
work and family to assist me; and to Florane and Sasha
Cyrelson for their emotional and financial support.

Table of Contents

Please Take Note

If you have purchased this copy of *GREAT TIPS,*
feel free to highlight or underline sections
of special interest and to use the following pages
for your notes, thoughts, and personal reminders.

If this copy has been loaned to you as part of
a work-related training program or a school course,
please do not write in any part of this book.

Use the supplemental worksheets provided by
your instructor for taking notes.

The Right Job For You?

"If there are 200 people in a room and
one of them doesn't like me, I have to get out."

Marlon Brando

Not everyone can or should be a waiter or waitress. Here is a quick quiz to measure how well you might do as a food server. No pencil necessary. Simply read each question and answer "Usually", "Sometimes", "Always", or "Never".

Can you take criticism without blowing up?

Can you stay positive when things go wrong?

Can you handle rejection without giving up?

Can you keep your cool in emergencies?

Can you laugh even if the joke is on you?

If you answered most of these questions with "Usually", "Sometimes", or "Always", congratulations! A good dose of self-confidence is important to your success as a server. But just because you answered "Never" to one or two of the questions does not mean you can't wait tables. People are not born with a high sense of self-esteem. They develop it over time. You can too.

Ready for the big bonus question? Please answer with a "Yes" or "No".

- *Can you see yourself approaching a table full of strangers, introducing yourself, and starting a conversation?*

I

If you answered "No", you are in the majority. Surveys have shown that the number one fear in America is "Speaking in Public". "Visiting the dentist" is number two and "Fear of death" is usually ranked number three.

In the upcoming chapters you will learn a variety of powerful techniques for dealing with stage fright, increasing your self-confidence, and maintaining your sense of humor; but if you had several "Never's" in the quick quiz and your answer to the bonus question was a loud "No!", it might be best for you and any potential customers if you considered working in a different field.

> What if you had several "Never's"
> but are already working as a food server?
>
> Don't panic! Help is on the way.

You are still reading so I will assume you have not been scared off yet. Waiting tables is hard work so I will try one more time to discourage you. Here is the down and dirty side of restaurant life:

As a waiter or waitress you will work weekends and holidays. You will have off when all your friends are working. You will be required to do mindless chores (sidework) every day. An incredibly rude family will request your station every day of their vacation but won't tip. You will burn your arm on the warming lamp. On some days your feet will hurt. On most days your back will hurt. Your clothes will smell. You will drop a plate of food in the middle of the restaurant, in the middle of a rush, when your nerves are totally frazzled. And then, just as your shift is about to end, the manager will ask you to stay and work a double.

Still with me? Fantastic! Even with all of that, food servers all across America believe that waiting tables can be one of the best jobs in the world.

Some of the benefits:

Job Satisfaction. Knowing that what you are doing is important. As a part of the waitstaff, you are vital to the success of the restaurant.

Instant Gratification. You will earn it in the form of bills, coins, and compliments.

Freedom. This book and your experiences in the restaurant industry will sharpen your sales strategies, time management techniques, and relationship skills. Valuable tools you can take anywhere.

Peace of Mind. Imagine you have to wait on a foursome that is both rude and cheap. A constant thorn in your side for 40 minutes. But once they leave, you can wipe down the table, re-set it, step back, and take a deep breath. It's almost as if that last party never happened.

Financial Security. U.S. News & World Report and Newsweek magazines ranked "food service" as one of the top 4 fields for employment opportunities until the year 2006. You will not become a millionaire waiting tables but you can almost always find work.

As one waitress told me, "On one side of me lived a guy who worked at the plant. On the other was a manager of some kind. Well, the plant re-located and the manager's company "down-sized" him. They both had to move. And me? I raised two kids and now own my house just working here in the diner."

Handling The Interview

"Every restaurant's goal is to make a profit.
For that to happen, the customers must enjoy their
dining experience and tell their friends."

Please read that quote again. Now close your eyes and say it out loud. You might feel a bit foolish but try it anyway.

Experienced waiters and waitresses know that at the heart of excellent customer service is an understanding of those two simple sentences. Committing them to memory will improve your performance on job interviews and increase your income when you become a server.

In this chapter you are going to get some powerful techniques for handling your initial restaurant interview but your willingness to learn those two sentences can mean the difference between success and failure. Take the time to learn them and then let's go on.

Most interview guides tell you to just act naturally during the interview. Don't. Not if you want the job. (The reason has to do with "Real Interview Question # 3" which we will get to in just a moment.) To be hired as a server, your comments and actions during the interview must show that you understand the next three important points:

Point one is that the owner or manager interviewing you wants to know three things before he will be comfortable hiring you. Whatever small talk or questions he asks will be his way of getting your answers to "The Real Interview Questions."

Point two is a rather rude reality. No one will hire you because you need a job. The exception to this rule is your family. If someone in your family owns a restaurant, you will probably spend some time working there whether you want to or not.

Point three is the logical conclusion: Restaurant owners and managers will hire you if you can show them you are a "Yes" to "The Three Real Interview Questions."

The Three Real Interview Questions

#1   Do you understand the restaurant business? (Remember those two sentences from the beginning of this chapter?)

#2   Will you do what it takes to make it happen?

#3   Do you fit in with our team and our image?

News flash! Your job interview does not start when you are escorted to the manager's office. It starts the moment you walk into the restaurant. So before you fill out the application, before you say anything to anyone take a quick look in the mirror. Does your appearance say you could fit in as a part of this restaurant staff? Your look should show that you could blend in with the waiters and waitresses you see at that restaurant.

You want to be neat and clean when you go on any type of job interview but this is especially important when applying for work in a restaurant. After all, you will be serving food and dealing with customers. Be sure your hands are washed, hair done neatly, clothes clean, and shoes shined.

The right appearance does not always mean suit and tie or your best dress. If you are applying for a summer job in one of the great roadside diners on the outskirts of Oklahoma City, a short-sleeved shirt and slacks or a simple summer dress might be more appropriate. If you are applying for work in one of the "gothic" restaurants in New York City, think ripped fishnet stockings and combat boots.

You want your appearance to suggest, "I belong here. I fit in with your restaurant's image. I should be part of your team."

Assuming you have a look that matches your target restaurant, your first goal is to get five minutes with the person who makes the hiring decisions. You are not there just to fill out an application or drop off a resume. Restaurant life is very people oriented. Getting a job in a restaurant is no different than working there. You start by talking face to face with someone you probably don't know.

Let's imagine you have selected a restaurant. You have reviewed and practiced the interview exercises at the end of this chapter. In your pocket you have a pen and the names and phone numbers of three people who know you and could honestly say some good things about you. You are dressed to fit in with the place, so you approach the Hostess. The conversation that might go something like this:

You: "I ... (recently moved into town, have lived here all my life, ate here the other day) ... and would like to work here as a waitress. Can you direct me to the right person?"

Hostess: "Sorry. There are no openings."

You: "I understand. I am really interested in a position here. Maybe there will be something soon. Who would I see for an application and a quick interview?"

Hostess: "Here's an application. Fill it out and it will be kept on file for the manager."

You: "Thanks. I appreciate your help. Could you tell me who would be the manager that I will talk with?"

Hostess: "Her name is Barbara Smith."

You: "Thanks again. You have been great. I am really interested in working here. Is it possible to talk with Ms. Smith for just three minutes?"

Hostess: "All right. I will page her."

Are you persistent? Absolutely. Smart waiters and waitresses know they are not entitled to anything. They work hard and get more because they earn it. That starts with getting the job.

Let's try another restaurant. Maybe this time there is no one at the door when you arrive. You wait patiently in the entrance until a waitress sees you, grabs a menu, and asks,

Waitress: "Table for one?"

You: "Not this time. I am here for the waitering position advertised in the paper. I would really like to work here. Who do I see for an interview?"

Waitress: "Henry. Wait here. I'll see if he is free."

You: "Thanks. I appreciate it."

Aggravation Saver

The decision maker will only have time to talk if the restaurant is not very busy.

Lunch hour may be convenient for you but it shows a busy manager you do not understand his business.

Although the 24 hour diner will not be busy at 4:00 am, is that the best time to ask for a job interview?

Choose a time that helps you make a good impression.

Whether you get resistance or help from the staff members you encounter, remember to remain friendly and polite. Once you get the job you will be working with these folks every day. Make a positive first impression.

Before you are directed to the manager or owner, you will probably be given a standard employment application. Fill it out to the best of your ability even if you brought a resume. (Smart servers always bring their own pen.)

Money Maker

You can not get a job as a waitress by mail.
No restaurant will hire you on the strength of
your resume alone. They will want to meet
you and talk with you.

Spend some time on your resume but invest more
time, energy, and effort on preparing yourself.

$ $ $

Don't worry too much about the "Work Experience" section of the application. If you have never worked in a restaurant, even if you have never worked anywhere before, just focus on the three "Real Interview Questions" and you will be fine. Restaurant owners and managers understand that waiting tables is often a "first job". Your attitude will be the biggest factor in their decision.

Let's continue. You have finished the application and are waiting patiently for the hostess to return. She arrives and tells you that the boss is free. She points you to a back booth where he is sitting.

Because most employers agree that they make the decision *not* to hire someone within the first five minutes of the interview, what you do next is very important.

Start by taking a deep breath. Yes, literally taking a deep breath. Oxygen feeds the brain. Helping you to think more clearly. Now for the rest of your body. You may know that your emotions influence your posture. Well, it also works in reverse. Your posture can alter your emotions. So when you take that deep breath, stand up as tall as you can. Shoulders back, chin level, and hands relaxed.

As you inhale and straighten up, a mood shift will automatically occur. You will begin to feel more capable and confident. Try it now. Wherever you are. Stand up (or sit up) strong and tall as you take a deep breath. Notice how you instantly feel more alert and aware.

This is a good time, while you are calm, to think about the interview from the Decision Maker's position. Since most restaurants do not have a Human Resources Department, the person doing the hiring usually has many other things to do. He does not want to spend day after day interviewing people. Since you are his next applicant, he hopes you are "the one." His goal is to find someone who can do the job and he wants that person to make money. Whether the Decision Maker seems like a nice guy or a grouch, he wants you to make money. Every restaurant manager knows that if you are getting great tips then the customers are happy. If his customers are happy then his restaurant will be profitable. Everybody wins.

With that in mind, as you start walking back to the boss visualize him giving you a bag full of money. Hopefully, thinking of the boss handing you a bag of money will give cause you to smile.

If everything is going according to plan, you are heading back to talk with the boss, walking tall, with a smile on your face. Pause as you approach him, look right into his eyes, and in a clear voice introduce yourself:

"Congratulations on opening your new restaurant. My name is Matthew and I would like to help make your new place a great success."

"Good afternoon. My name is Bill. I've heard great things about this place. I've come to join the team."

"Hello. My name is Barbara. I understand you are looking for someone to take good care of your customers. I am ready, willing, and able."

Think about what you could say before you reach the restaurant but don't over-rehearse. You want your words to sound natural, not like lines from a script.

Thinking ahead will also help you through the next phase of the interview - Questions and Answers. You want to listen carefully to each question then attempt to answer in a way that shows the Decision Maker you are a "Yes" to his "Real Interview Questions."

Whenever you are asked a question, it is wise to remember "The ten second rule for idiots and geniuses":

"An idiot tries to answer the question in ten seconds.
A genius waits ten seconds before he answers."

Here are some of the standard restaurant interview questions. If you think about them you will realize that they are the "Real Interview Questions" in disguise. After you read the answers given, think about how you could answer these questions.

"Tell me about yourself."
"Why do you want to be a waiter/waitress?"
"What are your strengths and weaknesses?"

Possible Answer: "I am the type of person who enjoys the highs and lows of dealing with people. I like the comfort of an established routine mixed with new challenges. Working here would give me all of that and I would give my all to your customers."

"What kind of experience do you have?"
"We get crowded. Can you handle a mob?"
"You have no experience. Why should I hire you?"

Possible Answer: "I understand every restaurant's goal is to make a profit. For that to happen I've got to insure every customer enjoys eating here and says good things about your place. I am ready to do everything in my power to make that happen."

"Describe your ideal job."
"Why do you want to work here?"
"How much money do you need to make?"

Possible Answer: "I am looking for the type of job where creating happy customers is rewarded. Each table is a chance for everyone to win. The customers have a great time. The restaurant makes money. And I get the tips and satisfaction on a job well done. I want to do that as often as possible."

Now it's your turn. Read the sample interview questions again. Think about how they relate to "The Three Real Interview Questions" and the goal of every restaurant. Can you adjust the answers in the book to fit your situation and personality? Can you create your own answers?

Always answer interview questions honestly but take the time to choose your words carefully. How you tell a story can make a big difference on the listener. You will only get one interview in this restaurant but if you think before you speak, one is all you will need to get the job.

After you have answered two or three of the Decision Maker's questions, take a deep breath, look the interviewer in the eyes and say, "I would really like to work here. How am I doing?"

Listen carefully to the Decision Maker's answer. A good manager will be honest and tell you his impression of your strengths and weaknesses.

If he decides not to hire you, don't lose hope. Interviewing skills take practice and time to develop. Learn from this experience and you will be better next time. If he tells you something like, "So far so good," be sure to smile and say, "Thank you."

During the interview you may have a chance to ask questions. Use it as an opportunity to gather information and give the Decision Maker some positive ego strokes. Everyone wants and needs recognition and appreciation.

Here are two great questions you can use when talking with an interviewer:

"How did you get started in this business?"

"What is your favorite thing about the restaurant business?"

Aggravation Saver

Don't worry about the low salary.
Waiters and waitresses are usually paid
next to nothing in salary.

Your income will come from tips.

If you practice the techniques in this book,
the tips will be enough.

New On The Job

"The readiness is all."

William Shakespeare

Motivational speakers and self-help books preach, "Attitude is everything." It's not. Some people say, "With a positive attitude you can overcome mountains." You can't.

The right attitude _combined with the right actions_ can and will give you incredible results. You need to learn the right actions; in this case, the actions that will lead to your success in the restaurant.

You need to learn what to do, how to do it, and when to do it. Then you need to practice until you are so capable and confident of your part that you can begin to focus on others (your customers). That's when you will really start to make money and have fun!

The good news is that because you are the new kid on the block, you don't need to be embarrassed by what you don't know. Everyone on the staff knows you are new so don't try to fake it and pretend you know it all. Take advantage of your "newness" to ask lots of questions. This is the one time you can ask anything and everything. So ask, and listen when they answer.

The best servers in the country agree with the old Chinese proverb, "Success happens when preparation meets opportunity". From your very first day on your new job, start preparing for success.

Even for experienced food servers, starting in a new place is usually a learn-as-you-go situation. Absorb as much information as you can as quickly as you can.

Don't waste your time re-inventing the wheel. Seek out the best waiter or waitress in the place and learn from him or her. Learning how to do each job the right way will become very important when you become busy.

New waiter or experienced pro, everyone makes mistakes from time to time. When you make a mistake, admit it immediately. If you owe someone an apology, sincerely apologize and move forward.

During your first week in the restaurant you will become acquainted with where things are as well as the policies and procedures you are supposed to follow. However, there are some things that will be true in every restaurant:

Choking and Heart Attacks

Choking is the sixth leading cause of accidental death. Sooner or later it will happen in your restaurant. Taking the right actions can save a life.

If someone appears to be choking, whether he is one of your customers or not, immediately ask, "Are you choking?"

If the person is coughing weakly, making high pitched noises, or is unable to speak, breath, or cough forcefully, offer to help. If there is another staff member nearby, have him or her notify the manager and phone for help while you begin the Heimlich Maneuver.

The Heimlich Maneuver

1.   Stand behind the choking person and wrap your arms around his waist.

2.   Make one hand into a fist and place it slightly above his belly button. Cover your fist with your other hand.

3.   With a quick, strong motion pull in and up.

4.   Check the results. Repeat the thrust in and up again as necessary.

5.   Once the food is dislodged, have the victim see a doctor.

Everyone should learn both the Heimlich Maneuver and CPR. Contact your local chapter of the Red Cross for information on when the next CPR course will be offered.

General Medial Emergency

While one person gives care to the injured staff member or customer, another server should call for help. Dial 911 or the local emergency number. Be sure to tell the dispatcher the location of the emergency, what happened, and what seems wrong.

Do not hang up the phone until the dispatcher hangs up. The dispatcher may need more information or may need to give you some instructions.

Language

Restaurants have their own language. Keep your ears open for the words and phrases that are particular to your restaurant. Some phrases can be confusing. Some words you may not know how to pronounce. If you are not sure, ask, or you may end up as one of my co-workers did.

It was her first dinner shift as a waitress. The kitchen chalk board said, "86 lobsters." Her first table was a party of four. She did a great job describing the lobster. Three took her recommendation. She proudly walked into the kitchen, erased the "86" and wrote "83." She turned around when she heard the explosion of laughter from the entire kitchen crew behind her.

Language lesson number one: If something is "86" it is unavailable. Take the time to learn the language for your restaurant. If you don't know, ask.

Payment

Some restaurants only accept cash. Some take four different charge cards, personal checks, and even have VIP accounts where customers simply sign the check and receive a bill at the end of every month. Learn the procedures for your restaurant.

If customers give payment to you, learning how to handle your "Bank" is very important. Talk with your supervisor until you are sure of how the transactions are to be handled. You may be the best waitress in the place and the customers may love you; but if you are consistently missing money, you will quickly find yourself unemployed.

Pouring

When pouring water, wine, coffee, or tea, try to avoid lifting the customers glass or cup. If the table is crowded and you must pick up a glass, hold it by the stem. For cups, keep the cup on the saucer and lift them both together by holding the saucer.

Whenever possible do not reach across the table to fill a glass or cup. Walk around the table rather than reach across.

Aggravation Saver

Never allow a customer to hold the coffee cup while you are re-filling it. The risk and potential danger are too great.

Repairs

Waiting tables can be a rough and tumble job. Keep a survival kit handy. Fill it with whatever could be important to you. Many experienced servers suggest you always have a toothbrush and toothpaste, some mints, make-up essentials, aspirin, deodorant, needle and thread, safety pins, Band-Aids, shoe laces, nylons, and a comb or hair brush.

Ladies, decide before the shift starts - either all of your nails polished or none of them. Having only seven polished nails is very distracting and gives the customer the wrong impression about you.

Money Maker

There are specific guidelines for how and when you can deduct the cost of buying and maintaining work uniforms. If your restaurant requires a uniform, you may get a tax break. Ask an accountant in your state.

$ $ $

R.I.C.E

This stands for Rest, Ice, Compression, Elevation. It is the right combination for treating most minor muscle strains and sprains. Use it on ankles, elbows, hands, etc. The faster you apply it, the better.

Start by taking all weight off the injured joint. Try not to move it. Apply an ice pack to the affected area for 15 to 30 minutes. Wrap the area to help restrict swelling. Raise the injury above the heart if possible. (Treating an injured ankle by sitting in a chair with your injured leg resting on another chair is not adequate elevation.)

After you have given the R.I.C.E treatment, check for a fracture. The signs of a fracture include a sudden and severe swelling, pain at the ends of the bones, noticeable deformity under the skin, or a loss of function in the injured area. If you suspect a fracture consult a doctor.

Serving

The rules never change: Serve food from the customer's left. Serve beverages from the customer's right. Clear everything from the customer's right.

The problem is that restaurant lay-out and design do not always make the rules easy to follow. Sometimes following the rules will be impractical. Sometimes it will be impossible.

If you are working the counter, all of your customers will be seated across the counter. It would be an incredible waste of time to walk around the counter just so you could serve from each customer's left or clear from her right. Likewise, when four people are seated in a booth there is no way you can get on the correct side for the two closest to the wall.

Successful problem solving will often follow the Marine principle of "Adjust, adapt, overcome". Smarter servers keep the rules in mind, follow them when they can, but do what it takes to get the job done.

Sick at Work

Most virus and flu "bugs" are very easily passed from person to person. For the sake of your co-workers and customers, call out sick if you have a contagious disease. Even though there is no way of knowing who got what from whom, it's not kind to customers or co-workers for you to go to work if you know you will infect others. Take the time to fully recover, restore your strength, and then go back to work when you are well.

Sidework

Yes, some tasks are mindless but that does not mean they are unimportant. Checking the silverware on each of your tables is neither complex nor difficult but you can easily imagine the impact on your tip if one of your customers picks up a spoon and discovers a lettuce leaf wrapped around the handle. As is often the case in the restaurant world, the problem may not be your fault but you will get the blame (and a lower tip). Do your sidework.

You can use the time spent doing your opening sidework to think about which of the techniques in this book you want to practice; or to create a new way to describe an appetizer; or to figure out why your reflection on one side of the spoon is upside down.

After a busy shift, use the time you spend doing your closing sidework to unwind. As you reset the tables remind yourself that the customers have gone. They have left the restaurant. Now allow them to leave your mind.

Table Set-Up

Here is the set-up for a rather formal meal. It includes virtually all of the utensils you will encounter. The proper sequence for use is from the outside in toward the plate. Learn this set-up and then modify it to suit your restaurant.

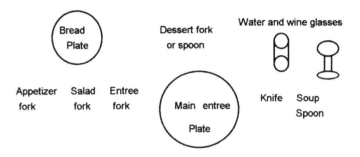

Money Maker

Go to work with a lighter, a corkscrew, a pen,
an extra pen, and an extra (extra) pen.

$$$

Money Maker

Do not bring an expensive pen to work.
It is highly likely that it will get misplaced or taken.
It may also give your customers the impression that you
have lots of money and don't really need a big tip.

$ $ $

Getting Along With
Your Co-Workers

You may be a good waiter. You might be a great waitress. But the time will come when you need some help. At that moment, the relationships you have developed with your co-workers will make a big difference. More importantly, the relationships you have with your co-workers will greatly influence how you feel about coming to work every single day. A bad relationship is like sand in the machine.

To create a good working environment for yourself and your co-workers think of the serving crew as a team. Try to be a "team player." When something goes right, share the credit. When something goes wrong, take the blame. Your co-workers will appreciate it.

Whenever you can, use phrases that help you to establish a positive relationship.

"May I?"	Asking permission shows respect and consideration.
"I'd like your advice."	Suggests wisdom.
"I'd appreciate it if ....."	Implies the person you are asking has the power to grant your wish.
"You are right."	Everyone enjoys a sincere pat on the back.
Please.	Always helpful.

Here are some common restaurant relationship problems and some possible solutions:

Hurt Feelings

People often say or do things without thinking. If one of your co-workers makes you angry or hurts your feelings, give him the benefit of the doubt. He may not have intended to hurt you or even thought what he said or did could hurt you. As soon as possible, explain to him very clearly how he hurt your feelings. You can prevent him from getting too defensive by starting your explanation with, "I'm sure you are not a mean person but it really hurt my feelings when you said ...."

Most people will apologize when you tell them something they did hurt you. If he apologizes, accept graciously. Some people will try to minimize the importance of the comment, or make it your fault by saying something like, "Hey it was no big deal. Can't you take a joke?" If he tries any of those strategies, simply respond by clearly re-stating your position, "When you say things like that it hurts my feelings. Please stop."

Aggravation Saver

Quick solution: Ask the person who made the remark, "Are you trying to hurt my feelings?"
This is especially effective if you ask when others are around. The question shines a spot light on Mr. Put Down and that is often enough to prevent any further problems. If he continues, he is a jerk and revenge may be justified.

Bad Moods

It happens. You wake up and just feel grumpy. Unfortunately you were hired to play the part of a cheerful and optimistic server. The boss is counting on you. So are your co-workers and customers. With the exception of a few restaurants in New York City and Los Angeles, waiters with bad attitudes do not get big tips.

Here are a few things you can do to brighten your mood:

1.   Acknowledge that you are in a bad mood but don't beat yourself up about it.

2.   Spend a few minutes thinking about the cause of the bad mood and some possible solutions.

3.   Call a friend. A five minute complaining session can help get some troubles off your chest.

4.   They say music soothes the savage beast. When you feel like a beast try your favorite music.

5.   Dance, take a short walk, or if you are in good shape try more vigorous exercise to trigger the creation of endorphins, promoting well-being.

6.   Deep breathing combined with gentle stretching can reduce the stress and tension that often result in a bad mood.

7.   Enjoy nature. A sunset, the ocean, leaves crunching underfoot have all worked to lift the spirits of your fellow servers.

Bus Staff

Talk with the manager about what he expects the Bus Staff to do. Are they responsible for getting water? Bread? Clearing plates? Re-setting tables? Also talk with the head waitress to learn what the servers expect from the bus staff. You may find the waitstaff view differs from management's. Trust the head waitress and you will probably avoid playing the "But I thought *you* were going to take care of that" game with your bus person.

The bus person is tipped by the server he or she is assisting, usually 10% - 20% of the total tips the server received. Find out what the standard payment is for your restaurant. Of course the amount you can count on your bus person and the caliber of the job he does for you is directly related to the amount you tip him. If there is any question on how much you should tip, round up. That extra dollar will do more for you if you give it to your bus person than if you keep it in your own pocket.

Money Maker

Some members of the bus staff may try to get away with giving you only part of their attention while they focus on earning side-tips.

Explain that you will both make more money if he gives every customer his full attention rather than just the select few he thinks may side-tip him.

$ $ $

Communication

Most problems between co-workers are the result of bad communication. If there is a misunderstanding, assume the message was not clearly received before you assume the other server is wrong, is out to get you, etc. It is rare that a fellow server will deliberately disregard a request. People who become waiters and waitresses are usually very accommodating to the wishes of others. Have patience. Your awareness that something you said may have been mis-heard or that something you heard was not what was intended will go a long way in preventing minor incidents from becoming major problems.

Covering

From time to time we all need a little help. Someone you work with may be dealing with problems and pressures that temporarily prevent her from doing her share. There is nothing wrong with doing a co-worker a favor or helping a friend. Offer to listen and try to arrive at an arrangement that works for both of you. However, no one should expect your help in doing something that is illegal or puts your job in jeopardy.

Gossip

Be very careful when you make a negative comment about a customer or co-worker. One more time. Be very careful when you make a negative comment about a customer or co-worker. Restaurant work can be very frustrating but negative comments have a nasty habit of coming back to bite you.

This would be a great time to introduce you to three food servers who just might be co-workers of yours. Please get aquatinted with "The Gossip," "The Critic," and "Holy Harry."

"The Gossip" considers herself a fountain of information; providing the important service of keeping everyone up to date and well informed. The problem is that her "information" tends to be only half true, often much less. Her gossip is usually just a negative spin on what someone else thinks might have happened.

"The Critic" has no interest in waiting on customers but has lots of time and energy to voice her opinions on anything and everything. A favorite topic is "How so-and-so screwed up." Stick around this character long enough and she will probably tell you what is wrong with you.

"Holy Harry" definitely knows what is wrong with you. In his world, the line is very clear between right and wrong, good and bad. This character is happiest when he is telling someone else how to live. Though his own life may not be filled with happiness and success, he is quite sure he knows how to run yours.

The best way to handle these characters is to keep a smile on your face and your teeth together. The less said to them the better. Though they may try to bait you, do not be lured into one of their traps. The conversation may start on a friendly tone but with these three it will rapidly deteriorate into something negative.

"Hello" and "Good-bye"

Once you have been working in the restaurant for a few weeks, you might not feel like saying, "Hello," or "Good-bye" to every staff member every day. To avoid offending your co-workers, use their actions as a guide. Some will greet you every day. Some will not. After you have worked together a while, it is okay to respond accordingly.

"Mr. Lazy"

As a group, waiters and waitresses are extremely hard-working. But every now and again you will find a server who consistently does less than his share.

Imagine you are working the counter in a popular diner. The morning rush is on. Customers are coming in for breakfast. They need to eat and then head off to work. You understand that waiting on more people means more tips so you are handling your half of the counter like a pro. You are giving customers good service but you are getting them fed and moving them out. Increasing revenue for the restaurant and yourself. On the other half of the counter "Mr. Lazy" just seems to be poking along. He's moving so slowly it seems like he still has the same customers from the beginning of the shift. What should you do?

Nothing. That's right, nothing. According to servers who have experienced this situation, your boss probably knows which servers are hustling and which are not. As long as you are not in a situation that requires you to rely on "Mr. Lazy" too much, keep your comments to yourself. Concentrate on doing the best job you can. His not turning over tables will probably give you more customers and opportunities for more money. Have faith that he will soon be looking for another job.

But what if you and "Mr. Lazy" are supposed to split all the tips from the counter? What if he never seems to make coffee or do any of the other tasks you rely on him to do so you can do your job? Then you must deal with the situation directly.

First, make sure you have your facts straight. If you are busy and feel a bit out of control then it is easier to think that a server who appears calm is calm because he is not handling as many customers as you are. That might not be true. The easiest way to get an accurate count is to review the number of checks and customers the two of you handled for the shift. Assuming the facts are on your side, begin by talking with him. Save him any embarrassment by finding a moment when the two of you are alone. Explain your position. You can prevent his becoming too defensive by saying something like,

> "Everyone has bad days and I guess you are just not into work today. The next time we work together I need you to do your part. I'm counting on you. The customers are counting on you. The boss is counting on you. Will you help me?"

This request should get you a positive response and a better workmate. If you do not see a change for the better, you have an obligation to the restaurant, the customers, and yourself to discuss the matter with your boss. Don't feel you are stabbing "Mr. Lazy" in the back if you discussed it with him first and gave him the chance to change.

Offensive Language and Dirty Jokes

Take it from waitresses who have worked in motorcycle bars and late night joints, you don't have to use foul language or tell dirty jokes to be liked and accepted by the staff and customers. That does not mean restaurant people never curse. They do. Often. I worked in a place with a Swedish head chef, an Italian second-in-command, and a Puerto Rican broiler man. On some nights there was profanity in all three languages. But it was only heard by the staff, in the kitchen, and that is the only place it can happen.

If you drop a plate of food in the middle of the dining room, both you and the manager may be thinking in language that would make a sailor blush; but if there are customers around, keep it on the inside.

Most people understand what profanity is and agree it is not acceptable in the workplace. What is "offensive" is often harder to define. A person who might never think of insulting someone outright may tell a joke that is racist, sexist, or in some way offensive to others. That old saying, "Sticks and stones may break my bones but names will never hurt me," is backwards. Sticks and stones cause temporary bruises. Words often have a more powerful and longer lasting effect.

That does not mean you can't joke around. Not all jokes are offensive and seeing the humor in a situation is a necessity for restaurant workers. Humor will sometimes be the only thing keeping you and your co-workers sane.

Learn at least one clean joke. It should be easy for you to remember, easy for you to tell, and should be at least a little funny. Ideally, it should appeal to children as well as adults. Here is an old stand-by:

A pickup truck goes speeding by. The police officer turns on his siren and goes chasing after it. When the pickup pulls over, the police officer sees that the back of the truck is filled with live penguins. He tells the driver that he will not give him a ticket If he takes the penguins right to the zoo. The driver say, "Okay," and off he goes. The very next day the policeman sees the same pickup truck, still full of penguins, go speeding by. He chases after it, pulls it over, and says to the driver, "I thought I told you to take those penguins to the zoo." "You did," the driver replied. "They had a great time. Today we're going to the beach."

Money Maker

Do not put your money or your job at risk by saying something that might be offensive. If you have any doubt as to the appropriateness of your joke or your comment, keep quiet.

$ $ $

Sex

Stay out of someone's private life unless you are very clearly invited in. Questions about preferences, sex, and other personal activities are just rude. And don't bore others by bragging or complaining about your own sex life. Those on staff who are not close friends, as well as any customers within earshot, do not need to hear what is or is not happening in your bedroom.

Though it might be important to you, most of your co-workers will not really care whether you are straight, gay, or if your current lover is a Buddhist kangaroo. Even co-workers who are good friends don't suggest sharing sexual secrets while at work. You will be better off saving personal remarks for get-togethers outside the restaurant.

Secrets

You will make some close friends working in the restaurant and while it is great that friends want to share personal information, work is not the best place to talk. Maybe the design of restaurants enhances the acoustics or maybe it's because waiters and waitresses tend to have exceptionally good hearing; but somehow, even secrets that were told in a whisper have been overheard and gotten out. Don't risk it.

Aggravation Saver

It's an old rule and a good one. No matter how tempting, never get into a physical/sexual relationship with your boss or supervisor.

Sexual Harassment

What you say and how you touch someone could be grounds for a lawsuit. Keep sexually oriented comments to yourself. If you must touch someone to guide her or move him, keep the contact within a "safe" zone. For example, the part of the arm between the shoulder and the elbow is a "safe" zone.

Suggestive Behavior

Whether you are asking a favor from a co-worker, customer, or the boss, be careful that how you ask does not lead to trouble when the time comes to repay the debt. It is only fair that if someone does you a favor he or she can expect one in return so do not imply or suggest something you are not willing to do. If you flirt with someone to get what you want you may find the repayment price is very high.

Theft

Sometimes it is easy to tell right from wrong. Using a customer's charge card to order that amazing thing you saw on late night TV is clearly wrong. A guy who steals food from the restaurant dumpster to feed his kids is not so clearly wrong. Don't steal from the restaurant or a co-worker unless it is worth over $100,000.00. Court cases in America have proven that unless you steal big, it is just not worth it. If you really want a pair of those great Pina Colada glasses, ask your boss. Odds are that he will either give you two or sell them to you at his cost.

Aggravation Saver

Two "Never's"

Never take the last of the coffee without making more.

Never take another server's food,
even in the mad rush of Mother's Day.

(Toasted English muffins are especially sacred.)

Getting Along With
The Kitchen Staff

Two quick truths:

1.   If there is a serious conflict between a good waitress and a bad cook, management will probably fire the good waitress.

2.   At some point you will have a conflict with the cook.

Most conversations between waiters and waitresses seem to eventually get around to that age-old restaurant question, "Why do cooks dislike waiters and waitresses?"

No server has the absolute right answer. Some think it is biological, a flaw in those who grow up to be cooks. Some servers think cooks resent servers. Busy or slow, the cooks make the same salary. When they see us coming it means they have more work to do. Others believe cooks view waiters and waitresses as live conveyor belts. That it is their culinary talent that is solely responsible for all customer satisfaction and that by rights all tips should be given to the cooks. Some suggest it is the feeling of power cooks get when they hear a waiter beg for the rest of his order or the thrill they get from watching a waitress break down and cry under a barrage of harsh comments. Some think it might be jealousy since cooks watch the servers go through the shift looking calm, cool, and clean while they spend the time juggling orders, wrapped in a grease cloud, standing next to a 400 degree oven.

Whatever the reason might be, it is important that you do everything in your power to maintain a positive, or at least professional, relationship with the cooks in your restaurant. Your ability to deliver an enjoyable dining experience and to earn a great tip are directly linked to your ability to get food out of the kitchen on time and prepared correctly.

Here are five sure-fire things any server can do to help maintain a positive server/cook relationship:

1. Don't eat from the customers' plate.

2. Know what you want to say before you start talking to the cook.

3. Don't eat from the customers' plates.

4. If you must talk with the cook, get to the point.

5. Don't eat from the customers' plates.

(I realize there are some repeats on this list but it was created by a group of cooks and we know some of them aren't that bright.)

Survival Tip

Never argue with someone holding a big knife.

Getting Along With The Boss

Restaurants have a written and an unwritten power structure. While it is important to know your restaurant's regional manager, district supervisor, general manager, assistant managers, and head waiter, it is equally if not more important to know who is dating whom, who are best friends, and who are mortal enemies.

Of course the most important person to you will be your boss. The VP of Operations may be the most important person on the corporate chart but in many restaurants you will hardly ever see him. The most important person in your world is the person you answer to every day - your boss. The key to getting along with your boss is to discover what is important to him or her.

How do you learn what is important? Well, as the great baseball coach Yogi Berra once said, "You can observe a lot just by watching." Start with the obvious - dress and behavior.

Is your boss more "spit and polish" or "rumpled and relaxed?" Does she start the staff meetings on time or is she always running a few minutes behind? Does she have any quirks or private passions? (Loves to play golf? Collects owls?)

If she walks the walk and talks the talk about cleanliness being next to godliness then all your efforts to be seen as a good waiter will be next to worthless if you show up for work in a dirty uniform. Likewise, if she is ready and waiting five minutes before the staff meeting is scheduled to start, you better not be late for your shift.

Keep your eyes and ears open. Knowledge is power. The more you know, the better your relationship with the boss will be.

Money Maker

You will get the "better" stations and parties if your boss thinks you are doing a good job. Let others tell him.

It may happen once an evening or only once a week but you will have a table where everything "clicks." The food came out on time and tasted delicious. The customers liked you and you did a great job serving them.

When you present the check, use a gentle sincere voice to ask if everything was all right. When you get a, "Yes," say, "I enjoyed serving you. If you had a good time too, please mention it to the manager or hostess on your way out. I am being evaluated and would really appreciate it."

Positive words from customers are a sure fire way to reach a manager's heart.

(If you are wondering about the truth of saying you are being evaluated, believe it. You are being evaluated on every shift. Don't think so? Just screw up.)

$ $ $

You may find it easier to understand what is important to your boss if you understand his "type." Restaurant managers tend to come in four basic flavors - Analyticals, Directors, Expressives, and Agreeables.

"Analyticals" are fact-oriented. They tend to speak in numbers, look to the bottom line, and demand accuracy.

"Directors" are more task-oriented. They are concerned with what is happening, how well things are progressing, and whether something can be accomplished without any problems or delays. They desire efficiency and "can do" responses.

"Expressives" are the dreamers of the restaurant world. They speak from the heart, want you to see their vision, and expect you to feel their passion. Talking with this type about day-to-day problems can be tough. They are often lost in how it could be and prefer not to deal with how it is.

"Agreeables" are relationship-oriented. They want everyone to be happy and to get along. If you bring this type a problem be sure you can suggest some solutions.

Even if the only contact you have with your boss is limited to the few seconds it takes for him to ask, "How are you doing?" and for you to respond, by understanding his "type" you can tailor your response to give him the information he desires; thereby making his question and your response a positive, relationship-building exchange.

Does your boss fit into one type? More than one? Which answer would build a positive relationship with him when he asks, "How are you doing?:"

"Great. My check average is up."   (Analytical)

"Great. I'm right on top of it."   (Director)

"Great. The customers love it here." (Expressive)

"Great. I really enjoy working here." (Agreeable)

Delivering Bad News to the Boss

Someone once said, "Problems are normal." If that is true, restaurants may be the most "normal" places on earth. If you are the one chosen to bring a problem to management's attention, it may be some comfort to know the boss is probably already aware of the situation. Never underestimate a good manager's intelligence or her ability to see and hear what is going on in her restaurant.

But what if something comes up and you are pretty sure the boss is not aware of it but should be?

In a perfect world the boss would be grateful to the employee who tells him about a problem as soon as it occurs, but that is not usually the case. Too often restaurant managers direct their feelings of anger and frustration toward the messenger. Soon the workers avoid delivering any type of negative news. The problems multiply and increase until a crisis develops. The boss is informed of the crisis. He explodes on the messenger and the cycle begins again. Trapped in such a cycle, the workers, the boss, and the customers all lose.

There is a way to deliver bad news, even to a difficult boss, that will get the information across without your having to don protective body armor or fear for your job:

Step 1. Gather all the facts, not just your opinion or what one person said happened.

Step 2. Gather support. If you are speaking on behalf of others be sure you talk with them before bringing the problem to the boss so you can be sure they share your view.

Step 3. Pick an appropriate time to tell him. Try to find a few minutes when you can have his full attention (and hopefully when he is in a good mood.)

Step 4. Lay out the facts. Don't be defensive or arrogant. If the problem is your fault, be up front about it.

Step 5. Focus on the situation, not on placing blame. This is especially important if the boss is the root of the problem.

Step 6. Suggest some possible solutions.

Problem Bosses

There are two types of bosses that require special care: "Volcanoes" and "Bulldozers."

"Volcanoes" explode unexpectedly and throw the adult version of a tantrum. Their first response to a problem, a threat to their authority, or any frustrating situation is to blame others - loudly! This is the type of manager who will yell at you in front of customers. The "Volcano" usually leaves his victims feeling humiliated, frightened, and angry.

Here is an effective strategy for dealing with this type that will keep you from being embarrassed in front of your customers and co-workers, and prevent you from becoming a victim too often.

As the "Volcano" begins to erupt, stand up as tall as you can, look him straight in the eye, and then bite down hard on your lip. For the first thirty seconds, keep silent no matter what he says. Let him explode. "Volcanoes" usually run out of steam pretty quickly.

When he slows a bit, make a statement that lets him know you appreciate the importance of the problem. Include a sentence to shift the conversation to a more private location and then move.

"I recognize this is important.
I would like to talk about this but not this way.
Can we discuss this in your office?"

Then turn and walk straight to the office.

When he arrives at the office, let him know immediately that you were not trying to undermine his authority,
"I know this is important to you
and I'm sure you did not want to embarrass
the customers by yelling in front of them."

Then ask for his view of the facts.

He may still need to blow off some steam but once you have created a break in a "Volcano's" outburst by changing the location, he will usually go from roaring lion to manageable pussycat. Continue the conversation but listen more than you talk. He is probably going to blame you. This will be especially tough to hear without responding in anger if he is blaming you and you believe he is really the cause. Try and keep cool. Since his explosion was out of proportion to the problem, your conversation may fizzle out. Nothing will get resolved and you can look forward to another explosion in the future. But if you stay calm and patient, he just might get past his own feelings and address the problem, might ask you for input, and might even work out a solution.

"Bulldozers" go right over people, their feelings, and often the facts. "Bulldozers" tend to make snap decisions based only on the information available at the moment.   After a decision has been made, they do everything possible to prove they were right., regardless of what the facts may indicate.   This boss is usually a fine example of that old saying, "Don't confuse me with the facts. My mind's made up."

It is very important that when you stand up to a "Bulldozer" you do not feed into an escalating war these folks love.   Your goal is to appear strong without being threatening. Not an easy task.

Think fact not emotion.   Here are some great opening phrases you can use when confronted with an on-coming "Bulldozer:"

"In my opinion ...,"   "I believe ...,"

"I disagree with you because ..."

Then quickly add as many appropriate facts as possible. Hopefully before he makes a rash decision.

It is vital that you follow up your statement of the facts with a phrase that shows the "Bulldozer" you recognize his intellect and importance. Something like,

"... but tell me more about what you are thinking."

As the conversation continues, try to get the "Bulldozer" to sit down. It's tougher for him to fight. But whether he sits or stands, you should remain standing and maintain eye contact. Expect a "Bulldozer" to interrupt, maybe even threaten you, when you try to speak. Don't respond to the interruption with a lecture on politeness or a verbal challenge. That will only escalate the battle. The best tactic has proven to be a simple, "Joe, you interrupted me," and then calmly continuing.

"Bulldozers" are usually task-oriented "Director" types who have gone temporarily berserk. Unlike the "Volcano" who explodes simply because he feels threatened or frustrated, the "Bulldozer" tends to roll over people because he wants the problem solved NOW. You can assist your "Bulldozer" boss by giving him all the information you have. Choose your words carefully and be sure to leave out as much of the emotional side as possible.

Once a problem is solved, don't be surprised if he wants to be friends. If you handle a "Bulldozer" the right way, you will earn his respect.

Aggravation Saver

Effective phrases to use with any type of boss:

"As of course you know ..."

"I'd like your advice."

"I'd sure appreciate it if ..."

"You are right."

Why Is Customer Service So Important?

"You can have everything you want
by giving enough people what they want."

Zig Ziglar

"Customer Service" is made up of all the words and actions that influence each customer's dining experience. If there is adequate parking, the greeting by the hostess, the cleanliness of the restaurant, the quality and quantity of the food, and the skill of the server are just some of the factors involved. Some you can control, some you can't.

The Alcoholics Anonymous prayer for serenity certainly applies to those who work for tips:

"God grant me the courage to change the things I can,
Accept the things I can not,
And the wisdom to know the difference."

One of the things you can change is where you work. If you really feel there are serious problems with a certain restaurant, move on. It will be easier for you to go to work every day if you actually like the place. And you will make more money with a positive attitude.

Once you have found a restaurant you feel good about, get to work. Waiting tables may not be your profession but for as long as you have the job you should think of yourself as a professional. Learn all you can about giving superior service. Focus on helping the restaurant make a profit by doing everything you can every day to insure all your customers enjoy their dining experience.

Why give so much energy and effort toward customer service? Why is customer service so important?

As a waiter or waitress the majority of your income is not going to come from your salary. It is going to come from tips.   Right now your tips are spread across the world, waiting for you in the pockets of the people who will become your customers. Each shift an unknown number of them will walk into your restaurant. Some days it will be hundreds. Some days it may be only two. But each shift a number of customers will come into the restaurant with money for you in their pockets.

That does not mean you should lure them into a back alley, hit them on the head, and empty their pockets. The goal is to have them give you the money voluntarily. They will give it to you if they feel you have earned it.

Please take a moment to re-read that last sentence. You need to be very clear on this point. It does not matter if you feel you have been working your tail off for the couple at table two. It does not matter if all your co-workers believe you qualify for sainthood because of how you handled that incredibly rude family in the third booth. Your customers will base the tip on how they feel about the total dining experience.

There are dozens of techniques and phrases in the upcoming chapters that you can use to influence how a customer feels. Each of these will strengthen your ability to provide good customer service. But with every customer, you basically have three options:

1. Give lousy service and hope for a tip;
2. Do the minimum necessary and deserve a minimum tip;
3. Give superior service and earn a great tip.

Testing by waiters and waitresses on thousands of customers, in virtually every type of restaurant, has proven that giving superior service, doing all you can to make every customer's dining experience a positive one, is the most consistent method for earning great tips.

Of course there will be days you will not feel like giving your all. There will be days you will feel like doing as little as possible.   And yes, it is true that even if you give superior service and deserve a great tip, there is no guarantee you will get one.

Some things will occur that are beyond your control. If a busboy knocks over a water glass while clearing the table, the wet customer may reduce your tip.

But since you will only have a limited number of customers on each shift and your goal is to maximize your income, your best bet is to consistently do everything you can to help every customer enjoy his dining experience.

Money Maker

There is a direct link between how you view your customers, how you handle them, and how they respond to you. You will experience lower job-related stress and a higher income if you agree ...

Customers are not an inconvenience or interruption.
You are not doing them a favor by doing your job.
They are the reason you have a job.
They deserve your best.

$ $ $

A small improvement in your level of service can make a big difference. Let's say you are working five lunch shifts a week. You usually wait on 15 tables per shift, each with an average check of $20.00, giving you total sales of $300 per day. You have been receiving tips on the low side of average, about 12%, so you have been earning $36 per shift. Just by improving your performance enough to increase your tips 3%, up to 15%, you would earn an extra $9.00 per day; adding $45 dollars to your pocket every week!

Why is customer service so important? The first part of the answer is that the level of customer service you provide effects how your customer feels and how he or she feels is one of the two measuring sticks the customer uses to decide your tip.

What is the other measuring stick customers use to determine the size of the tip?   The size of the check.

Yes, some customers subtract the cost of wine or drinks when figuring the tip. Yes, some don't tip at all. But most customers tip an average of 12 - 15% of the total bill. By using the "Suggestive Selling" techniques in the upcoming chapters, you can increase the total bill for each of your tables. This increase in your check average will result in a higher average tip. And once again, small changes can make a big difference in your take home pay.

In our last example, you were selling an average of $20 worth of food and drinks to each of your 15 tables every lunch shift. By improving your performance level, you were earning 15% tips which gave you $45 per day in tips, for a total of $220 in tips at the end of the week.

Let's say that selling just one more beverage and dessert per table would add approximately $4.00 per check. Persuading your customers to buy that beverage and dessert would increase your average $20 check to $24.00 and of course your customers would be tipping on this higher total. Earning a 15% tip on this higher check would add 60 cents to your tip for each table. True, 60 cents does not seem like much. But a 60 cent increase in the tip you earn from each of your 15 tables per day, for each of your 5 shifts, puts another $45 in your pocket at the end of the week!

Money Maker

Just by improving your customer service skills so your tips went from the low side of average (12%) to average (15%), and improving your sales skills so your average check total went from $20 to $24, you increased your take home pay (tips) by $90 per week. Imagine how much you could earn by giving superior service and having superior sales skills!

$$$

Besides your earning more in tips, something very important happened in our last example. Thanks to your sales skill, the customers purchased additional beverages and desserts. You know that restaurant owners and managers have made sure the prices for each item on the menu include just a bit of profit. Some items, like beverages and desserts, are usually more profitable than others. By directing customers to certain items on the menu, and by generally selling more, you will help the restaurant make more money. That additional profit allows them to stay in business and insures you have a job for another week.

Why is customer service so important?   The second part of the answer is that customer service includes suggestive selling; suggestive selling increases restaurant profits which in turn allows you to remain employed.

The third and final part of the answer is that customer service is your responsibility and obligation. Out of all the applicants, you were hired. Out of the thousands of restaurants in this country, these customers picked yours. Whether by chance or divine intervention they were seated in your station. They deserve your best.

Give them what they deserve and you will earn everything you deserve.

First Impressions

Because you with be dealing with the public, and most importantly, because you will be handling food, good grooming and hygiene are a necessity for servers.

No matter what type of restaurant you work in, five star or burger joint, there is a dress code for employees. In the section on job interviews, we discussed the importance of fitting in with the restaurant's image. You agreed to do so when you took the job. Now is the time to follow through on that promise.

The night before your shift be sure your uniform is clean and ironed. Go to sleep early enough so you will wake up refreshed and recharged; your eyes bright and your mind clear. Before dressing, shave, shower, and shampoo. Use just enough make-up to add to your appeal.

Because waiting tables is hard work, you can leave the house smelling good and looking sharp but by the middle of your shift your uniform may be less than sweet-smelling and more than a bit stained. Take a minute during your shift to check yourself over. It is just as important for you to look fresh and clean for your twenty-first customer as you did for your first. If the image in the mirror is looking more than a little rumpled, grab your survival kit. A few quick touch-ups can make a world of difference.

Now that your image is in order, let's discuss your voice. As a server, your voice is almost indispensable. It is a very rare waiter who could work an entire shift without speaking to anyone. Make sure your voice is working for you, not against you. Many servers are unaware of their actual tone, diction, and language patterns; however, there is a simple exercise to learn how you sound to others.

Place a tape recorder with a blank tape near the most used phone in your home. The next time you call someone or receive a call, hit the "record" button. When you hang up, hit "stop." Tape at least five or six calls. You want at least twenty minutes of conversation on the tape. Once you have filled about one complete side of the tape, take the tape recorder into your room. Do not do the next step in front of anyone else. A little privacy will allow you to concentrate on the voice on the tape without feeling self-conscious or embarrassed about how you sound.

Play the tape a few times. Really listen to your voice. Is the tone pleasant or harsh? Can you hear emotional changes or is it monotonous and flat? Do you tend to speak loudly or very softly? Are the words lost and garbled or easy to understand? Are there lots of fillers? (umm, ah, ya' know) Turn off the tape. Think about what you heard. You have the power to change anything and everything you feel could be improved. Awareness of your speech habits, listening to others, and a bit of practice can make those changes happen.

If you actually do this exercise, give yourself a big congratulations! Using a tape recorder is recommended by sales trainers in virtually every industry in America, but few people actually do this exercise. If you are one of the few, congratulations. Your efforts will pay off.

Now that you have taken the time to fine-tune the sound of your voice, pay attention to the words you choose. Watch "cutesy" and slang expressions. By the time you hear them most "hip" expressions are probably out of fashion. Review the menu for your restaurant. Be sure you can properly pronounce any foreign or unfamiliar words.

In the first chapter, I mentioned that public speaking is the number one fear in America. As a server you will spend the majority of your working day doing what most people dread. Isn't that a cheery thought?

There are four key steps to overcoming a fear of public speaking:

1.   Prepare ... your appearance and your voice.

2.   Prepare ... by learning all you can about the food and about your restaurant.

3.   Prepare ... key phrases and suggestive selling
        techniques.

4.   Take your work seriously and yourself lightly.

The first three steps are easy to understand. The only tough thing about steps one, two, and three is that you must actually do the preparation to get the benefits. The only "doing" required by step four is a shift in understanding. Step four is about messing up.

It is very important for you to accept that accidents happen. You will forget something, drop something, or say something wrong. Everyone makes mistakes. It's just that in a restaurant, most of your mistakes will happen in front of other people.

You will not die. Even though some people say, "I was so embarrassed I could die," death rarely comes. What does happen to some people is that they get so afraid of making an error they walk around the restaurant "dead serious." This puts their mind and body under tremendous pressure.

For your own health and well-being, and for the sake of your co-workers who need you to have a sense of humor to help them make it through the ups and downs of restaurant life, adjust your expectations and your attitude. Perfection is not possible.

Instead of spending your energy striving for perfection, do your best with each of the challenges that comes your way. This shift in attitude will prevent heart attacks, lower your blood pressure, and help you sleep easier.

There is an outstanding series of books and cassettes by C.W. Metcalf dealing with "Grace Under Pressure," and the importance of humor in our lives. They are available through the Nightengale-Conant Company (800-525-9000) and well worth the investment.

Timing

"Timing is everything."

Miyamoto Musashi

Have you ever said a silent prayer of thanks because you popped a mint into your mouth *just before* you ran into that gorgeous person? Or made a comment to a friend *just as* the person you were talking about walked up behind you? Or finally remembered the answer to a test question *just after* you handed in your test paper? If these or any similar situation has ever happened to you then you know that timing can make a big difference!

As a waiter or waitress, the difference between a good tip and a great one is sometimes just a matter of moments. Consider the difference ten seconds can make:

Situation one - Keeping a watchful eye on your tables, you appear just as the threesome make up their minds and put down their menus.

Situation two - You show up ten seconds later, after they have already begun to look around for you.

Good timing starts with being on time for your shift. Running late leads to bad attitudes - for you, your manager, and the co-worker who is waiting to turn over her station to you so she can go home.

Once you have figured out the best route to work and how long the trip takes, leave your house 10 minutes earlier than necessary. That way if something unexpected comes up, you have a buffer. If you make it to work early, use the time to learn something new.

Learn about a wine the restaurant sells. Learn how a sauce is made. Learn about the restaurant's history. Learn a new joke. Whatever you learn if fine. It is the learning habit that is important.

Money Maker

Ask how dishes are prepared.
Learn the ingredients in the different sauces.
Find out which entrees and sauces are prepared in advance
and which can be changed to accommodate a customer's
special dietary demands.

Learning about the dishes you serve will pay off.
Customers who have allergies or medical restrictions will
appreciate your ability to guide them through the menu.

$ $ $

Once your shift has started, whether you have two tables or twenty, if you do not manage your station it will very quickly begin to manage you. Correctly handling your tables will require your moving through the cycle of Pick up, Prioritize, Act, and Discard.

Watch the best servers in your restaurant and you will see that they make the best use of all their time, when they are in motion and when they are standing still, by constantly going through the cycle of Pick up, Prioritize, Act, and Discard.

"Pick-Up" refers to getting a new table or adding a task to your list of things that must be done.

"Prioritize" each item on your list. Ask yourself, "What's important now?" Some things must be done right away. Others can wait a bit.

"Act" on those high priority items. Find a way to get them done. Ask for help if necessary.

"Discard" or mentally cross a task off the list once you have completed it.

The best answer to, "How much time you should give a customer?" is "Just enough."

Give each party "just enough" time to settle in before you approach the table. Give your customers "just enough" time to enjoy their cocktails before you take the rest of their order. Give them "just enough" time to relax after their main course before you begin to clear the table.

To make things even more vague, "just enough" will be slightly different for each customer or party. It will require close attention and a bit of practice to understand the desires of your customers and to balance those desires with the number of customers in the restaurant, the capability of the kitchen staff, and the policies of the restaurant; and then, adjust your timing of the various courses to give a level of service that best accommodates all factors and satisfies your customers.

Here's a bit of bad news. The ability to handle a full station for an entire shift is not something you just wake up with one day. It takes practice. Unfortunately, most restaurant managers will not give you a lot of time to learn.

Do all you can to learn as much as you can as quickly as you can.

Initial Customer Contact

Most new waitresses and waiters view approaching a table full of customers as a dangerous situation. Restaurant managers often make it worse by telling new servers to pretend there are spotlights in the ceiling shining straight down on each table. That stepping into this ring of light is like stepping on stage and the customers are the audience. If the idea of being in the spotlight only serves to increase your nervousness, try picturing yourself as a tour guide. Imagine you are taking your customers on a trip through your world, your restaurant. As you gain experience and feel more comfortable with your skills, you will view each new party as a positive opportunity. Instead of a chance for embarrassment, you will see each party as an opportunity to earn more money.

Whether you are a new server or a veteran, take a moment as you approach a table to really look at your customers. What can you learn about each one? What do you already know? Is he a first time customer? Does this couple seem to be in a hurry? Are these three "regulars?" Does this party want you to provide entertainment or swift, silent service? Really seeing your customers, if you are focused and aware, will take only a moment but can give you the information you need to handle the party properly.

As you greet the customers, introduce yourself, and tell them about the specials (or whatever the procedure is for your restaurant), give your customers a gracious welcome. Use a warm tone. Make eye contact with each member of the group if possible. Pause for a second to connect with them. You will feel a more positive response from some members of the party. It is okay to play to your supporters. Talking to those who seem friendlier may help you to feel more relaxed and a relaxed mind functions better.

Remember that no matter how comfortable you get, even with "regulars," conversations about hot topics like politics and religion should be avoided. Your views may be reasonable and justified. You may even be "right." But why risk winning the battle and losing the war? (The tip!) Better to keep your opinions on any potentially controversial topics to yourself.

Here are some opinions that will have a positive impact on your income. Yes, some of these phrases are sexist and chauvinistic flattery but they have all been proven to be effective and the goal of this book is to help you get better tips not change the social fabric of our time. Use these as a basis for comments and compliments to your customers.

What a man likes to hear about himself:

That he is intelligent;
that he is well informed;
that he has a fair and logical mind;
that he looks tall and broad shouldered;
that he looks and acts like a wealthy man;
that he acts like he has a way with woman.

What a woman likes to hear about herself:

That her voice is pretty;
that her skin is smooth and glowing;
that her hands look like those of a young girl;
that she looks 3 - 20 years younger than she is;
that she wears her clothes like a movie actress
or fashion model (Avoid naming a particular
actress/model).

Money Maker

Men and women need and respond to positive emotional strokes. Don't miss these opportunities to help your customers feel good about themselves.
They will reward you for the ego boost.

$ $ $

Money Maker

Regular customers are great. They like you (despite their teasing). They tend to be tolerant when you are busy and they usually tip well. But they do want to be acknowledged as "Special." Taking that extra moment to make a positive comment acknowledging a regular customer pays off.

$ $ $

Even if you have known a customer for years, as long as you are depending on his or her tip as part of your income, there are some comments it is wise to avoid. Do not use the following as the basis for comments to customers:

What no man likes to hear about himself:

> That his language is poor;
> that he is getting old;
> that he lacks backbone;
> that he is a fool with women;
> that he can't hang on to his money.

What no woman likes to hear about herself:

> That she looks "tired;"
> that she has big feet;
> that she is putting on weight;
> that she is "well preserved" for her age;
> that you noticed some imperfection (varicose veins, moles, etc.).

There are almost as many ways to greet a customer, introduce yourself, and explain the specials as there are waiters and waitresses. If your restaurant has a set presentation, learn it and use it. If not, create the opening that fits your personality and your restaurant but be sure the opening you use covers all parts - greeting, who you are, the specials.

Here is an opening that has worked well for servers across the country:

"Thanks for coming in. My name is Lisa.
Before I take your cocktail order, I wanted to let you know that this evening we have two specials. They both look delicious. The first is ..."

Aggravation Saver

Experienced servers strongly suggest that you do not ask, "How are you?" unless you have a solid five minutes to listen. It is rude to walk away from someone who is giving you a run-down of her ailments and though five minutes is not a long time, it can feel like an eternity to a busy server.

Money Maker

You might have opportunities to assist customers as they arrive or as they prepare to leave by holding out a chair, helping someone take off or put on a coat, etc.

Take advantage of these opportunities to be of service. If you act with an attitude of courtesy then your assistance will be rewarded. But if your attitude implies the customers are a nuisance or an intrusion, they will pick up on it and it will be very hard to win them back (and get more than a minimum tip).

$ $ $

Alcohol

Alcohol is a multi-million dollar part of the restaurant business. Many people consider "having a drink," totally acceptable and an important part of dining out. If your restaurant serves alcohol, it is your duty to offer every customer of legal drinking age the opportunity to enjoy a beverage from the bar. If you have any moral or ethical hesitation in offering alcoholic beverages to customers, you will be better off working in one of the many restaurants that either by law or by choice, does not permit alcohol on their premises.

In a great many restaurants, approaching the table to take the cocktail/beverage order is the first contact a server has with a new customer. Use the opportunity wisely.

Try to gauge the mood of the party as quickly as you can. Is it a special occasion? Would champagne or a special bottle of wine be more appropriate than cocktails? Can you determine who is the leader, host, or hostess of the group? Can you get a sense of the timing of the party?

It is very important to know if the folks you are about to serve are over or under the legal drinking age for your state. You may not agree with the law but you have an obligation to enforce it. If it is even remotely possible that someone is underage, ask for proper identification. The penalties for serving a minor can be severe, for both you personally and for the restaurant.

Taking the beverage order

It is really quite simple. Just write down who gets what. Even if you are in a frantic rush, write down who gets what. Write the order as neatly and accurately as you can.

If you want to impress your customers with your great memory, write down their first drink order; then on the next round, you can sneak a quick look at the check before you approach their table and ask, "May I bring another (whatever they were drinking)?"

For even greater impact, memorize the customer's face and drink so when he or she returns to the restaurant on another evening you can say, "How nice to see you again. May I bring you a Chivas on the rocks with a twist?" (or whatever the drink was).

Be sure you understand exactly what a customer is ordering. Some of the things you hear are a bit odd - "Muddled" means to mash up the fruit in a drink.

Once you understand the special instructions, write them down. Taking the extra time to understand and write them down correctly is much easier than delivering an improperly prepared drink and having to do it all again.

Now might be a good opportunity to talk about how to take the order for any and every course.

Some restaurants have a positioning system for how checks should be written. For example, a common system is to designate the person in the chair closest to the front entrance as #1 and then go around the table clockwise. No matter which customer speaks first, second, etc., his or her order would be written on the line or area of the check that corresponds to his or her chair position at that table.

Using such a system enables you or anyone else to pick up that check and know who gets what. If your restaurant has a system, learn it and use it every time.

If your restaurant does not have an established system, you could work with the manager to create one for the restaurant or just use your own system for your station.

Whatever system you establish, use it every time on every table. Knowing who ordered what is especially important when you are busy.

Aggravation Saver

There are quite a few types of customers whose
behavior can create ordering nightmares.

There are those who insist on trying to order
while someone else is talking to you even though common
politeness and logic suggest it would be easier
if they ordered one at a time around the table.

But maybe the worst offenders are the ones who say,
"I'll have that too," when what they really mean is that
they want something similar.

Save yourself aggravation, time, and energy by repeating
the entire order to confirm that the second customer wants
exactly the same thing, "You would also like a vodka
martini, straight up, with a lemon twist?"

How you ask a customer what he or she would like
to eat or drink will definitely influence the answer you get.

Using what sales people call an "assumptive close"
can motivate a customer. Your tone and word choice
assume the customer wants what you are offering. For
example, the "assumptive close" can persuade a customer
who would have settled for water that a $1.50 ice tea is a
better decision:

"Sure is a hot one this afternoon.
I'll have a large ice tea for you in a sec."

Another suggestive selling technique, the "alternate
close," directs a customer's choice by asking the question,
"This or that?" To a customer who orders a beer, you might
say,
"Would you like a cold draft
or do you prefer your beer in a bottle?"

To use the "alternate close" successfully, you must know what your customers' options are. Take the time to learn which "top shelf" brands of alcohol are available and which appetizers and desserts are complimented by alcoholic beverages.

"Upselling" is simply giving your customers the option of a better quality product or a complimentary product. The results are a better dining experience for the customers, more revenue for the restaurant; and since the check total is one of the factors customers use to determine your tip, upselling usually results in more money for you.

Two examples:

"Would you like that vodka martini made with Stoli?"

"Our stuffed jalepeno appetizer would go perfectly with your margaritas. May I bring an order for the two of you to share while you are deciding on lunch?"

Here are two more easy ways to boost your check totals. First is the "Tie-down close." Simply use the customer's question to create the order. His own question ties down the sale.

Customer: "Do you sell wines by the glass?"

You: Certainly sir. Would you prefer Chablis, Rose, or Burgundy?"

The second easy method is the "Add-on close." The flattery used in the "Add-on close" places the customer up on a pedestal. The only way for him to gracefully get down is to add a bit more to the check by accepting your suggestion. To use the "Add-on close," you start your suggestion with the phrase,

"Unless I miss my guess, you're the type of person who appreciates something special."

And then make your suggestion.

With any "close," after you pop the question, be quiet. The answer will either be a "yes" or some type of a "no." A "yes" is easy. Simply write down the order. A "no" requires some thought.

Is it a definite "Don't ask me again" type of no? A "Well, maybe. Give me another push" type of no? Or does the "no" mean "Neither of those options appeals to me but I am open to something else. What else do you have?"

Tuning in to your customers and a bit of practice will enable you to hear the difference and know how to follow-up properly.

Money Maker

Sometimes the response to your question will be a "no" with an objection attached to it.

You: "That entree does not come with a first course but most folks like to start with a salad. Would you like a House salad or a Caesar salad this evening?"

Customer: "No. I only like hearts of lettuce."

If you can overcome the objection, in this case by getting her a hearts of lettuce salad (which is not on the menu), you will boost the check and have a grateful customer. Grateful customers leave great tips.

$ $ $

Whenever you are talking with customers, speak slowly and clearly. Turn your head and body slightly to include everyone with your voice and your eyes. But even this technique and speaking in a strong voice will not save you from the occasional customer who needs you to repeat whatever you just said.

Yes, it is annoying when someone asks you to repeat yourself because he was not paying attention. Yes, it slows you down and screws up your timing for the twelve other things you need to get done. But when it happens, smile, and repeat it all again in a slow clear voice. Patience pays off.

Money Maker

Whenever you are sent somewhere, to the bar for sodas, to the kitchen for desserts, etc., always ask your customers, "Would anyone else like a ...?" This type of question has "jump on the bandwagon" appeal.

By adding a phrase like, "... while I am headed to the bar," gives the question a sense of immediacy.

Sales people call this a "Better act now" close. Try it and watch your check average skyrocket.

$ $ $

Serving Drinks

If your restaurant uses "bar trays" (serving trays the size of a small pizza) for carrying drinks, you will need to practice before you can handle it without accidents. Balance in on your palm, finger tips, or for a more secure grip keep your thumb curled over the edge. Try adding empty coffee cups, then water glasses, working up to one half-filled wine glass. When you can move through the restaurant comfortable with the wine glass, you are ready.

Aggravation Saver

Gravity is a law! Removing drinks from only one side of a bar tray will create an unbalanced see-saw effect.

Whether you use a bar tray or hand-carry the drinks to your tables, remember the rules dictate that if possible you should stand on the right side of the customer and place the beverage on his or her right (above the knife).

Aggravation Saver

If a bar tray or a food tray becomes unbalanced and you are unable to regain control of it, let the tray fall to the floor. Crashing glasses, plates, and food on the carpet will not make the manager happy but it is far better for all concerned to let a round of drinks or a plate of clams in red sauce hit the floor rather than a customer.

Do not put your fingers inside the glasses to clear them from the table even if the customers have gone!

Some kids under ten will drink the entire soda the moment they get their hands on it. Give a young child's beverage to the parent and allow them to give it the child.

Money Maker

Experienced servers recommend serving a very young child's beverage in a takeout cup with a lid and straw. The parents will be pleased they have found a server who understands kids and pleased parents leave great tips.

$ $ $

Wine

The first upscale restaurant I worked in required servers to wear a tux. The first week, I was dazzled every time I got dressed for work. By the end of the month, I realized that the tuxedo was just a uniform. Likewise, wine is simply a beverage.

That may seem harsh to lovers of the grape but it is important to eliminate the hype and pretense surrounding wine so you can become comfortable suggesting and serving it. With that said, make wine a part of your on-going education. There is a quite a bit to learn and you get to drink your homework.

Here is some basic information to get you started.

Appetizer Wines

Dry and sweet sherry, dry and sweet vermouth, red and white Dubonnet, Lillet, and Campari are all good choices for a pre-meal drink. They are served chilled or "on the rocks."

White Table Wines

Soave (pronounced "Swa vay"), Verdicchio ("Ver dick ee o"), and Pouilly-Fuisse' ("Poolee Foo say") fall into this category. Chablis ("Sha blee"), the most well-known white, is named for the region of origin, the French province of Chablis. Other white wines, such as Chenin Blanc, Chardonnay, and Reisling, are named for the type of grape used in that wine and may come from anywhere. White wine is popular as a pre-dinner cocktail as well as a compliment to lighter fare. White and Rose wines should be served chilled.

Always hold stemmed glasses by the stems!

Red Table Wines

This group includes Burgundy (a region in France), Chianti, Cabernet Sauvignon (pronounced "Sa vin yon"), and Zinfandel. It is usually helpful to uncork a bottle of red wine approximately 10 - 30 minutes before drinking to allow the wine to "breath." This mellows the flavor of the wine and allows any unpleasant aromas to dissipate. These wines are served at "Room Temperature," which means below 70 degrees Fahrenheit, regardless of the actual dining room temperature.

Aggravation Saver

When you open a bottle of red wine to "breath,"
be sure you put it somewhere ...

Safe - so no one drinks it, throws it away,
or uses it for cooking

Obvious - so you remember it when the time
comes to serve it

A good place for a wine to "breath" is right on the
customer's table wrapped in a napkin.

Sparkling Wines

Sparkling Burgundy, Rose and Champagne are all in this category.   Serve them all very well chilled.   A sparkling wine is a terrific addition to any type of celebration. Chilling the glasses is a nice touch.

Here are two quick methods for chilling glasses:

1.   Fill the glasses with ice, add water until full.
Wait 60 seconds, empty glasses. They are ready.

2.   Carefully place the glasses upside down into the ice and water inside the Champagne bucket. Wait 10 - 15 seconds, shake dry. They are ready.

Aggravation Saver

Do not chill champagne glasses by burying them
in an ice maker or ice container.

They will get smashed and changing the ice is not fun.

Aggravation Saver

Even the finest champagne starts to lose
its fizz the moment it is opened. Check with your
customers so you know when they want their
bottle of champagne opened.

With cocktails so they can make a toast?
When you serve the main meal?
With dessert as a great finish to the evening?

Dessert Wines

Sweet Sauternes and Sherries are served chilled. Port should be "room temperature." Sparkling Asti Spumante and the sweet Champagnes are served very cold. All of these will complement the sweetness of most desserts.

Recommending a Wine

For years the rule has been, "The lighter the meal, the whiter the wine." White wines were automatically suggested for most chicken, fish, or veal dishes and red wines were suggested for meat and games dishes.

Today, many people disregard the rules and order a wine because they like it or because they recognize the name, regardless of whether the wine will complement the flavors of their meal. Wine experts and chefs may frown on such behavior but if your customers order a wine without asking your opinion, bring it.

If you are asked for a recommendation, you will need to know which wines your restaurant sells and which wines best complement each of the dishes your restaurant offers. Make time before a shift to talk with the head bartender, manager, or wine steward if your restaurant has one. You want to be able to recommend at least one high, one medium, and one low priced option for each dish on your menu.

Do not be shy in asking for help with wine recommendations. Servers have reported that more than once their asking questions about wine resulted in a wine tasting/training session for the staff.

Before you suggest a wine, think about the price range these customers are in. If they have ordered shrimp cocktails, Caesar salads, and lobster tails, they are more likely to go with one of your medium to high priced suggestions. (Recommending a wine is a good opportunity to use the "Alternate close," giving your customers the choice of "this or that".)

In the most formal dining rooms, it is appropriate to suggest a different wine with each dinner course. A formal luncheon has no more than two wines. Champagne, if ordered, can be served with any course and throughout any meal.

Opening Wine Bottles

Before you reach the table with the customer's chosen wine, use a cloth to wipe all dust and dirt from the bottle. Present the cleaned bottle by showing the label to the person who ordered the wine. When he or she nods to indicate "Yes, that is the wine I ordered," you are ready to begin opening the bottle.

Secure the bottle in one hand, against your body, or as a last resort on the table. Cut the foil neatly below the lip of the bottle and remove the cork using your favorite opener. Opening a bottle of wine is not a difficult task given the right tools and a bit of practice.

"Levers" are the traditional waiter's choice. They look like small pocketknives and are easy to carry. There is a blade for cutting the foil collar on the bottle, a spiral "worm" to insert into the cork, and a lever to pry up the cork.

Start by cutting off the foil. Press the blade against the bottle neck just under the lip (about 1 inch from the top of the bottle) and gently turn the bottle so you cut a full circle. Lift off the cut foil and slip it into your pocket. Place the tip of the "worm" in the center of the cork and with a slight downward pressure give it a good twist. Continue twisting the "worm" into the cork but do not press down. That might push the cork into the bottle. When about one bend is left showing on the "worm," secure the lever against the lip of the bottle. Pull straight up (not diagonally across the bottle's top). The cork will come out slowly and easily.

There are three other commonly used wine openers: Blades, Batwings, and Screwpulls.

A "blade" is a pair of thin steel blades which are wiggled down around the cork then all three are pulled up together. New servers tend to push a few corks into the bottle before they get the hang of a "blade" but once you master it, it's foolproof. You will never break a cork with a "blade." Unfortunately, "blades" lack pizzazz.

"Batwings" have even less pizzazz than "blades." "Batwings" are heavy, usually too big to fit comfortably into a pocket, and often don't work well on the longer corks used for expensive wines. The idea with a "batwing" is that once you have screwed the "worm" into the cork, you press down on the "wings" and the cork comes up and out.

"Screwpulls" are unquestionably safe and are the easiest to use. The plastic sides of the "screwpull" fit down over the bottle and most have extra long, extra thin "worms." Most restaurants now suggest their servers use "screwpulls."

Every time you open a bottle of wine, look inside the neck. A young wine may need only a quick pass of a clean napkin to insure cleanliness. An older wine can have a surprising amount of buildup on the cork and inside the bottle neck. Pouring wine over this grunge will not improve its taste. Take a moment to gently rub it off with a clean damp cloth before pouring any into a customer's glass.

If the cork is intact, present it to the person who ordered the bottle by placing the cork next to his or her wine glass. Place about two "shots" of wine into the customer's glass. A gentle twist of your wrist at the end of the pour will prevent a trail of wine drops across the table.

While the customer is making a big show of examining the wine in the light, checking the clarity, the "nose" (its bouquet of aromas), and its "legs" (how the wine runs down the inside of the glass), you should casually pass the wine bottle under your nose.

Wine that has gone bad smells and tastes like vinegar. It is very rare for a well-stored bottle to sour but if this is one of those rare occasions you want to find out before the customer tastes it. Drinking bad wine is about as much fun as drinking sour milk. Do your customers a favor and do your smell check before the customer does her taste test.

If you suspect a bottle has gone "bad," ask the customer to wait just a moment while you take the bottle to the manager, supervisor, or head bartender. If one of them confirms it is indeed sour, bring a new bottle to the table, apologize, briefly comment on the rarity of a bad bottle, and start again.

Occasionally, a dry or incorrectly extracted cork will break before it has been completed removed. This is not a crisis. Don't panic. Take a deep breath. Discard the broken half, re-insert the "worm," and with a gentle touch and a little luck the rest of the cork can be pulled up and out of the bottle.

Decanting

Sometimes bits of cork crumble and fall into the wine. This is not a crisis. Tell the table you will be right back, "I'll have this decanted for you and return in a moment," should be sufficient. Once out of the customers' sight, strain the wine through a wine strainer or clean kitchen strainer. In a pinch you can use a coffee filter, or as a last resort a clean napkin.

A broken cork is not the only reason to decant a wine. "Decanting" simply means separating the drinkable wine from the sediment at the bottom of the bottle. Very old wines, especially the substantial reds (Bordeaux's, Cabernet Sauvignons, Rhones, Barolos, and most of the vintage Ports) benefit from decanting.

If you need to decant an old bottle of wine, it will be easier if you have let the bottle stand upright for an hour (a day is even better).

Being careful not to shake the bottle or to stir up the sediment, uncork the wine and clean the neck. Hold the bottle over a flashlight, a light bulb, or a candle flame (Be careful not to warm the wine). The light is to enable you to see through the bottle so you can see liquid and the sediment. Once you can see, begin gently pouring the wine through the filter into a carafe. Smarter servers always use a light when decanting to eliminate any guesswork.

Opening Champagne Bottles

Opening a champagne bottle, like making a bank shot on a pool table, is easy if you use the right angle. But always treat a champagne bottle with respect. The pressure inside is roughly the same as the pressure in a large truck tire; about 90 pounds per square inch. A misdirected cork could cause serious injury.

After you remove the foil wrapping, keep your hand on the cork as you begin to remove the wire hood. You can either toss the foil and wire into the ice bucket or slip them into your pocket. With the wire hood removed, hold the bottle at a 45 degree angle and with a firm grip on the cork, slowly wiggle the cork up and out. Because a 45 degree tilt allows a greater surface area to the liquid inside so a greater number of gas bubbles can rise at the moment of opening, keeping the bottle at a 45 degree angle should prevent bubble over.

You may want to drape a cloth napkin over the cork, secure it with one hand around the bottle neck, and use your other hand to push up the cork.

Try to give the appearance of relaxed ease while you are opening any type of bottle for a customer. Remember that you are on stage. With practice, it will get easier.

Pouring Wine and Champagne

With the approval of the taster (usually the host or hostess of the table), begin pouring. In the most formal setting you would start with the woman on the host's right and work your way around the table.

An average bottle of wine will yield four to five portions. If you have four people sitting at a table, it is better to give slightly less than half a glass each the first time around the table. For dessert wines, only fill each glass one third full.

Turn your wrist in a gentle circular motion as you complete each pour. This will prevent a trail of spilled drops from glass to glass.

If someone switches types during the meal, bring a new glass. Never pour a red wine into a glass that held white or vice a versa. It damages the look, smell, and taste of the second wine.

A good way to sell the second bottle of wine is to pour the last few drops into the host's glass. This lets him know the bottle is empty and that his guests will not be getting any more unless he orders another bottle. This maneuver coupled with a questioning look from you will usually get that additional order. But you have to feel out your customers.

Even if they are drinking fairly quickly, there is a risk if you empty the bottle too soon. The host may not want to, or may be unable to, pay for another bottle. Running out in the middle of the meal, or even worse, before the arrival of the entree, could cause him embarrassment. If he feels embarrassed your tip will suffer.

Wine Spillage

It happens. Your fault or theirs, it does not matter. A glass of wine or an entire bottle has been tipped over onto the table. It may seem obvious but the first thing to do is turn the bottle up so no more pours out. Now grab some napkins to dam the flood and protect your customers. Once you have stopped the spread, give extra napkins to the customers so they may begin cleaning themselves while you finish cleaning the table, replacing wine covered utensils, etc. Be sure you alert a supervisor to the potential for customer complaints.

How to handle a "Bar tab"

Your customer is seated at the bar waiting for the rest of his party to arrive. He orders a drink, finishes about half of it, and his dinner companions walk in. He would like to take the drink with him to the table. What is your restaurant's policy for handling such a situation?

Does he pay the bar tab first? Is it transferred to the dinner check? How are tips for the bartender handled?

Good questions. Your supervisor has the answers.

Money Maker

If possible, get the beverages to the customers before they order their meal. Do everything you can to make sure they have them before any food arrives.

Not having a beverage to sip on makes waiting for food to arrive seem especially long and is a strike against you that is tough to overcome.

$ $ $

Serving The Meal

Let's go slowly through the serving process for a table to give you an overview of how and when certain things should be done.   Since this is make believe, we will assume everything will go wonderfully.   We will deal with customer complaints and problems in upcoming chapters.

The hostess has just seated your first party for the evening, a group of six. You greet them, introduce yourself, and make some suggestions for appetizers. You then take a cocktail order and head for the bar.

You deliver their drinks, tell them about the specials for the evening, and give them "just enough" time to settle in and make some decisions.

You return to the six, remind them of the specials, take their order and make appropriate suggestions for appetizers, soups, salads, and side dishes that would complement their meal and the over-all dining experience.

A quick note on recommendations: Be honest. The restaurant is in business because people keep coming in. There must be some items you can honestly suggest.

Maybe it's the tuna salad sandwich the secretaries all love. Or the split pea soup the truck drivers all request. Or the chocolate cake your daughter goes crazy for. Whether it is a crowd pleaser, a personal favorite, or a single customer's endorsement, if you have a reason to recommend something, do it.

Back to your party of six.   In the "old" days, a woman whispered her order to her husband or male escort. She was never supposed to talk directly to the waiter. Those days are gone. Women have found their voices and usually handle their own ordering. When you are taking an order, give the women in the party the respect they deserve by assuming they will order for themselves. Turn toward each lady to give her the option of speaking directly to you.

Money Maker

If a customer makes a request that you do not understand,
do not walk away from the table confused.
Politely ask her to explain what she wants.

Your time is valuable. Use it wisely.
By understanding the request you will make fewer trips,
have happier customers, and make more money.

$ $ $

Once all six have placed their food order, which you have written in an organized manner so you will know who gets what, pause for a moment before you leave the table and think about suggesting wine or champagne.

Both are terrific complements to food, add to the dining experience, and boost the check. Most managers have carefully chosen and priced wines and champagnes that work well with your restaurants style and menu.

Money Maker

Do not be afraid to make suggestions.
According to the Sales and Marketing Executives Board,
the #1 reason salespeople fail is their tendency to pre-judge
customers and decide in advance that they might not
or will not accept the suggestion.

Smarter servers pre-judge their customers and
come to the opposite conclusion:

Customers want to and will buy what you suggest.

$ $ $

Most cooks begin working on an order the moment it arrives in their hands. Your decision as to when to give the kitchen an order will depend on three key factors: The needs of the restaurant, the status of the kitchen, and the desires of your customers.

Restaurants are in business to make money. More customers in the seats means more money in the cash register. When your restaurant is busy, the boss will want you to "turn over" your tables - to give good service but to try and move the customers out as quickly as possible. You also want to take advantage of the busy times. The more customers you serve, the more opportunities you have to be tipped.

Unfortunately, food cooks in the same amount of time no matter how may customers are lined up outside the restaurant door. Even though most cooks will prepare as much as they can in advance, if your restaurant fills up at 12:10 and everyone wants to be finished lunch by 1:00 PM, the kitchen is going to be a very busy place for those 50 minutes.

When the kitchen is busy, you can help the cooks by giving them as much time as possible to deal with your order.

Your customers' desires should also influence when you place the order for each course. If they arrive at 7:00 for dinner and tell you they plan to see the 7:30 movie, you will need to tell the kitchen to put a rush on the order.

In our make believe world, the restaurant is not busy yet, kitchen is on top of things, and your customers are not in a rush. But just to make it interesting, let's imagine one of your six has ordered a well done steak.

You know that takes some time so you give the entire order to the kitchen immediately. They will begin on the steak and start the other dishes a few minutes later.

Since three ordered appetizers, that is the first course you need to serve. If someone on the kitchen staff is responsible for the hot and cold appetizers, go where you should be to pick up the first course and wait patiently. A good cook does not need to be reminded that you are waiting for an appetizer. He will put it up as soon as he can.

If you are responsible for getting the shrimp cocktail from the "walk-in," or for dishing out the soup, do what needs to be done. Do not forget the little touches - cocktail sauce for the shrimp, a soup spoon and crackers for the soup, etc.

When you have all the first course dishes loaded on your serving tray, or on your arm if your restaurant does not use serving trays, head out to the table. Place the tray down on the tray stand or "jack," pick up the first person's appetizer and serve it (from her left side if possible). Continue until all have been served their first course.

In a very formal setting you would start serving the appetizers to the woman on the host's right and end up with the host. Though this is socially correct, it is not always possible. The general guidelines are still, "Ladies first," and "Seniority has priority."

Giving your party of six just enough time to finish the first course and discuss how wonderful the appetizers tasted, you appear beside the table. You clear the first course dishes and silverware, take another drink order to refresh their beverages, and after delivering the drinks head off to the kitchen for their salads.

A quick note on clearing: Clear each appetizer from the customer's right side with your right hand, transfer the dirty dish to a side tray or, if you must, stack the dirty dishes in your left hand. In a formal setting, you would move clockwise around the table ending up by clearing the host last.

The salad course is placed directly in front of the customer. If the customer wishes to save his or her salad for later, or if it is served after the entree, the salad is placed to the left of each customer's dinner plate.

You serve the salads to your six, remembering because you wrote it down, to bring the lady in the #2 position her dressing on the side.

Your customers are almost finished their salads. You check with the kitchen. The cook tells you the steak needs about ten more minutes. You head back to the dining room. Two minutes later all six of your customers have finished their salads. You wisely give them a few more minutes before you clear the salad plates.

Money Maker

Customers are usually more comfortable waiting a few minutes for the next course if the previous course's dishes are still on the table. Having an empty table seems to make the gap between courses feel longer.

This does not apply if they have finished the last course and are waiting for their bill.

$ $ $

With only three minutes before the steak is done, you begin clearing the salad plates. Take advantage of any time between courses. Give customers another chance to order wine or a gentle suggestion to save room for dessert.

Two order a glass of wine but because *getting food to the customers while it is hot is a top priority*, you head to the kitchen since you know you can not get the wine from the bar and deliver it to the table before all six meals will be ready for you to pick up.

Because the members of a smaller party (less than ten) will usually wait for everyone at the table to be served before starting to eat, if it is possible, try to serve everyone in the party at the same time. Sometimes the kitchen does not make this easy to do.

If the cook tells you to pick up but only five of the six entrees are ready, ask how long before the last one is ready. If it will only be a few moments, deliver the five and hurry back to pick up the sixth, or have a co-worker run the sixth entree out to you while you are serving the five. If it is going to be more than a few minutes, see if you can keep the five dishes under the warming lamp until the last is ready.

Guests in larger parties are expected to start eating as soon as they are served so if you are handling a group of 10 or more, deliver the meals as rapidly as you can but never carry more than you can handle. It takes much less time to make another trip than it does to re-do a meal dropped on the floor.

No matter the size of the group, the cook has skillfully arranged the presentation of each plate. Your thumbprint in the gravy was not part of his plan. Keep your fingers out of the food.

After you have served the entrees, you can usually get a laugh from your customers if you present any necessary condiment (ketchup, jelly, oil & vinegar, etc.) with a great flourish as though it was the finest wine. The less snobbish the restaurant, the bigger the laugh.

The hostess has seated a party of two in your station. As you begin serving the couple you maintain gentle contact with your six top. Like a circling shark, you are always in the area; making it easy for your customers to get your attention. This involves your physically being "on station" and your apparent willingness to be of service.

The first part is simple - stay on your station! You can do yourself the least harm and the most good if you stay where you should be. The second part is a bit tougher because the customer can not read your mind. Even if you are sending full force mental messages directly to the man on table seven, it is unlikely that he will receive them. You must look interested and caring.

Start with the basics. Are you facing your customers or turned away from them? Are your arms folded? Are you leaning against a wall? Is your face projecting a "Don't even ask" attitude? Remember that your customers will tip based on how they feel. Do all you can to help them feel good about you.

When a customer speaks, pay attention. Listen to the customer's words, voice, and body language. If he says, "I usually get more potatoes with the meatloaf," you need to really pay attention to be able to hear if he is complaining about the quantity of the potatoes or a lack of attention and pampering.

A safe strategy is to acknowledge any request with a comment like, "I will do what I can." Then go do it.

If the news is good, break it happily. Use positive terms. Choose words that tell the customer the good news and at the same time remind him you have been working hard to serve him.

If the news is bad, tell the customer as soon as possible. Hesitating can lead to fear and avoidance; both will hurt your ability to provide good service and get a good tip. Eventually you will have to face the customer so tell him promptly using a three step report to minimize the negative impact of the news.

The three steps are: status report, explanation of "why," and the offer of an alternative. For example, if your customer ordered a dessert before you knew it was all gone you could report, "We are all out of strawberry shortcake. It is very popular. The rum cake is also popular and I think it's terrific."

Be generous when you can be. Learn what is permitted in your restaurant. Can you offer a coffee refill for free? Extra dinner rolls?

Your six have finished their entrees and you have given them just enough time to relax a bit before you arrive to clear the table.

Unless you are handling a party of 15 or more, wait until everyone is finished eating before you start clearing. For larger parties or if you are very busy, it is certainly acceptable to clear some members of the party as they finish eating. This partial clearing is recommended if you see customers stacking up their dishes.

If you are even a little unsure whether someone is finished eating or is merely resting, ask. Be sure there is no question as to whether she wants to "take home the leftovers."

All six in your party are finished with their entrees but you ask to be sure. One lady would like to take the remainder of her stuffed flounder home so you are careful not to put anther plate on top of her dinner.

In the kitchen you turn her dinner into a foil swan and return to the table to finish clearing. After clearing and crumbing the table you discuss the dessert options and ask if anyone would like coffee or tea. If your restaurant offers any coffee drinks, now is the time to mention them.

As they make their dessert and coffee selections, think about what after dinner drinks would compliment their choices.

Coffee is usually served in either a cup and saucer or in a mug. Fill the cup or mug only as full as you can comfortably carry without splashing. Place the filled cup and saucer or mug on the table to the customer's right. Do not hand a seated customer a cup filled with hot coffee.

When you give a refill, leave the cup on the table, pick it up with the saucer underneath. If your customer lifts the cup for you, gently take it from his hand. Hot coffee, and it should be hot, is never poured into a cup held by a customer. That is an accident waiting to happen.

Never very far away, you move back to your six when they have finished about half of their coffee. As you refill their cups, you suggest another after dinner drink or another dessert.

Yes, it is okay for people to eat more than one dessert. You occasionally eat more than one helping of dessert at your house. Shouldn't your customers have the same opportunity? You can sell additional desserts if you find a way to overcome the guilt your customers may have about ordering a second helping in public. Using a phrase like, "I can never have just one slice of the blueberry pie here," may do the trick.

Most people wait until after dinner before smoking. Know your restaurant's policy as to who can smoke and where.

Money Maker

To change a dirty ashtray, ask the customers to remove any lit cigarettes from the ashtray then place a clean ashtray on top of a dirty one. Remove both together from the table. Return the clean ashtray to the table while you keep the dirty ashtray covered by your hand as you walk to a trash can.

Be sure all fires are out before you dump the ashtray.

$ $ $

When your customers are completely finished with their meal, step away from the table. Prepare their check and return to the table.

Customers find it especially frustrating to finish a great meal and have to look for the server or wait for the check; even if it is only a short wait. If your restaurant is not computerized, carry a calculator. Taking too long with the check can ruin an otherwise perfect job.

Who gets the check? The person who asked for it.

If they ask for separate checks at the end of the meal, politely explain that you wrote everything very clearly so they can see who ordered what and for how much. Let them know you would be very happy to provide separate checks "next time" if they will let you know at the beginning of the meal.

Aggravation Saver

Be sure your writing is clear and readable!

The cook, your partner, the manager, and the customers may all have a need to read what you have written. Most importantly, you need to be able to read what you wrote. When it gets busy, you will not be able to remember it all.

Write it down and keep it clear.

Several courses that would be part of a more formal meal (the sorbet, etc.) have been left out of this meal but once you know the basic routine, adding in the rest is much easier. Take the time to learn the routine for your restaurant. Your efforts will pay off.

Clearing The Table

When the main course is finished, the rules for formal dining dictate that the customer place the knife and fork side by side on the entree plate with the sharp side of the knife facing the fork, which is to the left of the knife, tines up (American) or tines down (European). The knife and fork should be placed fully on the plate so they will not slide off when the plate is lifted. Unfortunately, you can not count on your customers to have read the rule book even if you work in a five star restaurant.

Your feeling for the timing of each table is the best guide as to when you should clear or move them on to the next course. If you have any doubts, be safe. Ask a "win/win" question:

"Are you taking a break (pause)
or may I take that plate out of your way?"

"Would you like a few more minutes to relax (pause)
or may I tell you about our dessert specials?"

Remember to follow the rules whenever possible: Serve food from the left, beverages from the right, and clear everything from the right. So to clear a course, you start from the first customer's right side, pick up the dirty plate with your right hand, and deposit the dirty dish in a convenient bus pan, serving tray off to the side, or if you must, stack it in your left hand.

Clearing a table takes practice. Eventually you may be able to clear six or more entree plates in one trip but never take more plates or glasses than you can handle. It is better to be slow than sorry. Remember that clearing a course means removing the dirty silverware from that course as well as the dishes but be careful to watch out for sliding silverware!

There may be times when you get busy and want to combine steps. To clear one course and immediately serve the next, you would begin on the first customer's right with your right side closest to the table and her entree dish in your left hand. Clear her dirty salad dish with your right hand, move around to the customer's left side and rotate so your left side is closest to the table. Place her entree dish in front of her. Now dispose of the dirty salad dish that is in your right hand, grab the next entree dish in your left hand and move to the second customer's right side. Clear his dirty salad plate with your right hand, move and rotate to his left side and place his entree in front of him. Dispose of the dirty dish in your right hand and grab the next entree plate. Repeat as necessary around the table.

Aggravation Saver

If there is even a possibility that the customer
may want to take something home, ask!

It only takes a moment and asking is much more pleasant
that digging through the bus pan or garbage can
for the rest of that steak.

Some of your customers may want to take their leftovers home. Here's how to make the tin foil "Swan".

To change a pork chop into a swan, start with a foot long rectangular piece of foil. Place the chop in one corner of the foil. Fold the chop inside the foil until you reach the opposite/diagonal corner. Pinch the foil as close to each end of this "tube" as possible and twist once at these two end points to seal in the entree. Now bend one end up to form the "tail." Roll the other end to form the "neck" of the swan. Bend the neck into an "s" and you're done.

Aggravation Saver

The foil swan will not work for "soupy" entrees.
For those you will have to use a container.

Return to the table with all of the swans and doggie bags and begin clearing all the side plates, the butter dish, bread basket, and dirty silverware. Make as many trips as necessary to be accident-free. As you clear, look around the table. Be sure each guest has a clean spoon for coffee and a clean fork for dessert. If not, be sure you bring one the next time you come to the table.

Once you have cleared everything, take a moment to "crumb" the table. You can use a butter knife wrapped in a napkin, or a professional "crumber," to clean the majority of crumbs and stray pieces of food from the table. Do not wipe them into your hand. Use a napkin, a plate, or a bar tray. While you are "crumbing" the table is a good time to ask if anyone would like coffee.

Aggravation Saver

If you are assigned to the coffee station,
be sure you stay on top of it.
All modern coffee machines and most of the older models
take less than three minutes to start a new pot.
Learn how to use the machine in your restaurant.
The coffee station is one job that if left undone, will
definitely become a problem for you and the rest of the
servers at the worst possible moment.

Money Maker

On breakfast or graveyard shifts, 99.9% of coffee drinkers want a cup as soon as they sit down. They will wait for everything else as long as they have coffee. Be sure and get these folks their coffee. Then, when you take their food order, offer a glass of juice. Most customers feel they "should" have juice, many will say "Yes" to the suggestion.

$ $ $

Telling your customers about the desserts your restaurant offers is another great opportunity to practice your suggestive selling skills.

Everyone likes dessert but in these health conscious times many people need to feel that they were talked into it. Use all the "sensation" words you can to describe your restaurant's various temptations. Tell them they "must" try them.

Sometimes there is no substitute for direct contact. You might try placing a dessert on the table "to help them make up their minds."

Aggravation Saver

Any time you need to speak with your customers,
walk up to the table and silently start counting to ten.
If you reach ten and still do not have their attention,
you can interrupt their conversation by saying
something positive like,

"Forgive the interruption but I wanted to
be sure you knew about the terrific specials
we have this afternoon."

or

"I am glad you are having a good time.
For dessert this evening ..."

Presenting The Check

In previous chapters we talked about the importance of being available to your customers and being aware of what is happening on your station. This is particularly important when customers finish their meal.

Customers find it especially frustrating to finish a great meal and have to look for the server or wait for the check; even if it is only a short wait. If your restaurant is not computerized, carry a calculator. Taking too long with the check can ruin an otherwise perfect job.

You know the host or hostess of the group is usually the one to ask for the check but if someone else asks, that is the person who gets it.

Money Maker

Presenting the check is a great opportunity
to strengthen the emotional bond between you
and the customer who is about to tip you.

Studies have proven that even a brief touch
can have a strong positive impact.

As you place the check on the table,
lightly touch the host's arm between the shoulder
and elbow and say, "It was a pleasure serving you."
A two second touch in this "safe" zone will dramatically
improve your tips.

$ $ $

You can eliminate most arguments concerning the check - arguments with you, the cashier, and between members of the group - if you take the time to write clearly.

If a party requests separate checks at the end of the meal, show them that the bill is clearly written so they can easily determine who owes what. Offer to provide separate checks the next time if they "remind" you at the beginning of the meal. If they still need separate checks, do what you can.

Sometimes customers ask for separate checks when what they really want are separate receipts (for individual business expense reports, etc.). Since it is usually easier for you to get check stubs or receipts than to create separate checks, ask. A polite question can save you time and effort.

Money Maker

My first waitering partner, Barry Chilkotowsky,
a master waiter and bartender, taught me this great
investment strategy for making your customers feel you
and they are special:

If your restaurant does not give out mints,
buy a bag of individually wrapped mints at the local
supermarket. When you present a check,
add a mint for each of your customer.

This is especially effective when serving
the breakfast or lunch crowd.

$ $ $

People Of Different Cultures

America has long been called, "the melting pot." If you tried, you could probably find someone born in every country on earth who is now either living in America or just visiting here. As more businesses become international and the availability of low-cost air travel increases, you can expect to see an even greater variety to the customers you will be asked to wait on.

As a server, your job is to help every customer that enters your restaurant feel comfortable. Those born outside the United States might look differently than you do, speak with an accent that is different than yours, and have different customs; but if they are in your restaurant, they can pay the bill and leave a tip and that qualifies them as a Customer.

You will do a better job as an ambassador for your restaurant and your country if you keep four important points in mind:

1. These folks are from another culture. They are not deaf or stupid. There is no need to shout or talk down to them. Speaking slowly and clearly will help you to be understood.

2. Listen carefully when they speak. Try to tune your ear to their accent so you can more readily understand them.

3. Ask questions often to be sure they understand you and you them.

4. You will probably need to repeat a question or piece of information more than once since you, or they, may miss it the first time. A smile and some patience will be rewarded.

Aggravation Saver

Tipping is handled differently in other countries and cultures. You may need to gently explain that ...

"A tip for service has not been added to the check.
Good service is usually rewarded with a 15 percent tip."

Said with courtesy, these two simple sentences
should prevent you from getting "stiffed."

Do not be embarrassed to make such a statement.
If you gave good service you earned the tip.

Children Are Customers Too

The bad news is that if the kids have a really bad time, the whole family may never come back. Since losing customers is not good for the restaurant, you need to know how to handle children.

One possible strategy is avoidance. You can choose to work in a restaurant that discourages parents from bringing their children. This will greatly reduce the number of kids you will have to deal with on the job.

But if you decide to work in a restaurant that allows or even encourages parents to bring their kids, you can take hope in the fact that eight year olds rarely pay the bill. It is the parents that you will have to impress.

The good news is that parents know kids are tough to handle in a restaurant setting. Almost every parenting book says that dining out with children is going to be a hassle!

Imagine how grateful the parents will be when they finally find someone (you!) who can help them enjoy a meal out with the kids. Learning how to serve kids without losing your smile will earn you loyal customers and great tips!

Experienced servers have found that parents who go out to eat with their kids tend to fall into three categories: "Watch dogs" who bark and control their kids all through the meal, "White flag wavers" who have completely surrendered and do nothing to control their kids, and the great majority of parents who fall somewhere between these two groups. Regardless of which group your customers fall into, they will expect you to get the job done without your losing your cool.

Here are some tricks you can use to make it easier:

Seat the family in a booth. This gives the kids wiggle room without disturbing other customers.

Bring the kids some crackers as quickly as you can. This will occupy their mouths for a little while.

If the children have a hard time settling down even after you have delivered crackers and their beverages, ask the parents if they would like you to bring the children's meals first. Be sure and ask. Sometimes feeding the kids first is a bad idea!

If the child's meal comes with any type of sauce or dressing, always serve it "on the side."

If the children have finished but the parents are still eating, maybe the kids would enjoy a little art. A paper placement or unfolded paper napkin can be his or her canvas. Add a crayon (from the jumbo pack you purchased at the local $1.00 store) and let them get creative. Remember to ask for the crayon back so you have one for the next child.

Use all available resources. Talk with the other servers to trade tricks and coping techniques.

The most important thing you can do for your restaurant, your customers, and your own piece of mind is accept that some of your customers will be kids. Acceptance will give you patience and sanity in what can be a most stressful and chaotic environment.

Money Maker

Never ever criticize a child in the presence of his or her parent. Parents know when their child is obnoxious. They may even be embarrassed by their child's behavior. But they do not want or need a stranger pointing it out.

$ $ $

Suggestive Selling

"In the beginning, words and magic were
one and the same thing. Even today,
words retain much of their magical power."

Sigmund Freud

Every day you do and say things to influence the attitude and behavior of those around you. You may be trying to get your child to clean his room, convince a prospective date to go to the movies, or persuade a customer to order the daily special. In these and countless other situations, you are using "suggestive selling." So let's get past the idea that "suggestive selling" is something foreign or that there is anything wrong with using these types of techniques. What is "wrong," is doing it badly.

The pushy salesman and the woman who bullies a friend into doing something may win temporary victories but he will lose the customer and she will lose the friend. To paraphrase Norman Vincent Peale, your goal is to influence people and win customers. The phrases and techniques in this chapter will enable to do just that.

With practice, you will be capable of swaying people's decisions to a degree you may not have thought possible. The secret is understanding how we make decisions.

Even though we like to view ourselves as logical, rational creatures, the truth is that the majority of our decisions are based on 85% emotion and only 15% fact. People decide on an emotional level and then justify the decision with facts. Therefore, the most effective way to influence people is to appeal to their emotions.

Describing the look, texture, sound, and taste of a dish will motivate 85% of the decision making receptors. Saying that it is on sale will influence only 15%.

Advertisers call this approach, "Right-brain marketing," because they target the right side of a person's brain, the side that controls emotions, when they use words and phrases that involve the senses or create an image.

Scientists have even determined that the right/emotional side of the brain or the left/logical side of the brain can be more directly accessed by speaking into the opposite ear. What to reach her emotionally? Stand on her left side and your whispered message has a better chance of reaching her emotional right brain and causing an emotional response. Want to appeal to his logic? Stand on his right.

The following phrases come from the field of Neuro-Linguistic Programming and the work of Milton Erickson. They appeal to the "right brain," the emotional side and the basis for 85% of our decisions. These phrases will work in the restaurant and with a little modification, will work in your personal life as well. Practice them often. The better you get, the more money you will make. Each of these phrases enables you to give the targeted person an embedded command. They are most effective if you speak in a gentle, clear voice. Used properly, your customers will follow the suggestions without perceiving you as "pushy."

"I'm wondering if ... "

> I'm wondering if you have ever tried ice cream on top of your pie. I'm wondering if you're hungry enough for the large size.

> You never told your customers to do anything. You were just wondering.

'You may ... "

> You may want to order an after dinner drink while you relax before dessert. You may want to try a different one of these phrases each shift.

> Give them permission. Tell them, "You may."

"Will you ... now, or will you ..."

> Will you order another round of cocktails now or will
> you enjoy these until you order the wine for your
> meal?

> Will they do this now or that later? It sounds like
> they have a choice but they really don't.

"One could ... because ... "

> One could think about ordering the large onion
> rings because you may not be aware of just how
> hungry you are.

> "Because" is the magic word in this phrase. It lends
> emotional credibility to whatever you say before it.

"Can you imagine ... "

> Can you imagine what you would do with the extra
> forty or fifty dollars a week in tips you earned by
> using these phrases? Can you imagine actually
> enjoying going to work?

> People are more likely to do something they are at
> least a little familiar with than something totally
> unknown. This phrase is a great way to get them
> thinking about it. Creating that familiarity.

"... said, "_____"

> Everywhere I go, waiters and waitresses say,
> "David, your book has been a great help!"   One
> server said, "Using suggestive selling phrases
> almost doubled my income."

> Quoting someone else allows you to deliver a
> message, give authority to a suggestion, or to say
> something that you could not say yourself.

"I could tell you that ... but ... "

> I could tell you that learning these phrases will give you more persuasive power but I would rather let you discover it for yourself. I could tell you that this phrase is a great way to avoid resistance when you try to upsell customers but you probably figured that out.

"You could ... "

> You could try a much better wine for only a few dollars more. You could order another dessert and not feel guilty about it.

> Of course your customers could. They have free will. Or do they?

"If you ... then ..."

> If you choose one the specials this evening then I am sure you will be delighted.

> This is a cause and effect statement but it doesn't have to make sense to be effective. To verify the "then" part, the customer has to do the "if" part, which is really all you wanted the customer to do anyway.

"Some people ... "

> Some people learn faster if they highlight important sections of a book. Some people have a desire to earn more money and reduce aggravation.

> The first thing every person does when he hears the phrase "Some people" is to check inside to see if he is one of those people. So use this phrase and give your customers something to check for.

"You don't have to ... "

>You don't have to understand how this works in order to use it with your customers. You don't have to think about cheesecake with your coffee.

>This is called a "truism." On the surface, it is a true statement and therefore can't be argued with. Beneath the surface lies an embedded command.

"Maybe you'll ... "

>Maybe you'll practice these embedded commands on your friends. Maybe you'll dream of hypnotizing your customers and taking over the world. Maybe you'll buy a copy of this book for your best friend.

>Who know? There is no pressure. I'm just saying that maybe you will.

My thanks to Robert Anue who created the fun and fascinating game of "Zebu." You can order your very own set of 52 Zebu playing cards because you want to learn all of the phrases and increase your income. Eventually you will want a set of cards. Call now. Zebu, the hypnotic language card game, 800 - 937 - 7771.

Money Maker

Your customer's name is the most important and most effective word you can use.

Learn the names of your regular customers.

$ $ $

This next group of phrases should be removed from your restaurant vocabulary:

"I don't know."

> If you don't know, find out. Smarter servers replace this phrase with, "That's a good question. Let me check and I'll find out for you."

"We can't do that."

> A great phrase if you want to really aggravate your customers. Smarter servers replace "We can't" with, "That's a tough one. Let's see what we can do."

"You'll have to ... "

> You are probably wrong. There are very few things a customer has to do. Try the phrase, "Here's what you can do ..."

Starting a sentence with, "No."

> This rejects whatever the customer just said. In most sentences, if you dropped the "no" the sentence would still be grammatically correct and would have a much softer impact.

"Sweetheart" or "Hon"

> Save the terms of endearment for your family, especially if you are waiting on a couple. Calling a man "sweetheart" or "hon" when he is sitting with a woman is a good way to make her your enemy, cause him unnecessary grief, and put your tip at risk.

Life "In The Weeds"

On some days everything goes your way. You move with grace and speed, all of your customers are generous, even the cooks seem friendly. Then there are times when everything seems to fall apart. The coffee pots are empty, the ice cream you need is locked in the freezer and you can't find anyone with keys, and you just can't seem to get to that new table. Welcome to life "in the weeds."

Being "in the weeds" is how servers all across America describe feeling overwhelmed. When you have too many things to do and not enough time to do them.

Don't Panic. Start climbing out of the weeds by taking a deep breath. Oxygen feeds the brain, helping you to think more clearly, and it energizes your muscles for the work ahead.

Now for the rest of your body, you may know that your emotions effect your posture. The reverse is also true. Your posture can influence your emotional state. So when you take that deep breath, stand as tall as you can. Shoulders back, chin level with the floor, and hands on your hips.

As you strike that pose, say (to yourself), "I can handle it." Two things will instantly occur. You will smile, which is always good in a stressful situation, and your mood will shift. You will begin to feel more capable and confident.

The next twenty seconds should be used to organize and prioritize what needs to be done. Slowing down for 20 seconds will seem like a ridiculously long time. You may even have to force yourself to take the full twenty, but do it. Plunging blindly forward is for fools.

For most restaurant, the top three priorities are:

1.   Get the food out of the kitchen and onto the tables, especially if it is hot food.

2.   Get checks to those who are ready to leave even if you have not cleared their tables.

3.   Greet the new customers and get them something (a beverage, water, bread, etc.).

Talk with your supervisor or manager to be sure that you know the top three priorities for your restaurant. When it gets busy it will be too late to ask.

A word of advice. When you take that breath and strike that pose, don't do it in the middle of the restaurant. I know and you know that you are taking a 20 second pause to organize and prioritize what needs to be done; but to the customers, it looks like you are just standing still and that can make impatient customers even madder.

Once you know what needs to be done, look around. Is help available? If so, don't hesitate to ask for assistance. Most people like to help. It makes them feel good.

If you have some help, quickly discuss "what's important now" so each person knows what he or she is responsible for and then get going. If no help is available, start with the top priority and just keep going. Eventually, you will get caught up.

Aggravation Saver

If you are really buried and your co-workers say
they are deep in the weeds and can't help you,
try the assistant manager or the manager.

He or she may be able to give you the three minutes
of emergency assistance you need to get back on top
of the situation again.

So many servers suggested asking the manager or assistant manager for help when you're in the weeds that I included it in the book. But an equal number of servers told me to warn you that assistant managers and managers tend to lose their cool faster than waiters and waitresses. When the restaurant is busy, the assistant manager or manager might be the worst person to ask for help.

When the restaurant is extremely busy and the dining room and the kitchen seem almost out of control, you must be on guard not to become swept up in the nervous energy of those panicking around you. To keep your head while those around you are losing theirs is not easy but it is possible.

Here are three strategies that will make it easier for you to keep your head, keep your job, and stay out of the weeds:

1.   Work efficiently. Deal with tasks in batches. If you are going to the bar for one table, see if you can get beverages for your other tables at the same time.

2.   Think with a pencil in your hand. If you want to remember something, write it down. This is especially important when you are busy.

3.   Reserve your work time for work. Don't sacrifice your mental time or emotional energy on problems or gossip not related to the job at hand. Leave your personal problems outside the restaurant door. They will wait for you, like a good dog, until your shift is over. But you will probably discover that focusing on work, on your customers, and on providing the best customer service you can, will result in your earning more money; and although money does not solve everything, it can go a long way toward resolving many of the problems you left outside the restaurant door.

Handling Customer Complaints

Customer:	"Waiter, I want some oysters. Not too large or too small, not too old or too tough, and they must not be salty."
Waiter:	"Yes sir. With or without pearls?"

Maybe it was your fault. Maybe it was completely beyond your control. Sooner or later one of your customers is going to complain. Here is a step-by-step strategy for handling most complaint situations:

1. Start with an open mind. The customer believes his complaint is justified. Whether it was your fault, his fault, or something beyond anybody's control, he feels he has the right to complain.

2. Do not get into an argument with him. You might win the battle but you will lose the tip and maybe even your job.

3. Actively listen. Instead of politely standing in front of him, dreaming about whacking him on the head with a plate, really listen. Tune in to what he is saying and how he is saying it. Active listening enables you to discover what you will need to know to resolve the situation.

4. Gather the facts. What happened? What part of the situation is the most upsetting to the customer? What does he feel should be done about it? You will probably find that the more you and the customer discuss the situation, the calmer he gets and the less he wants.

5. Repeat to the customer what you have heard. Be sure that what you are going to try to fix is indeed what he wants fixed.

6. Do everything you can to make it right.

7.   If it is not in your power to satisfy the customer, go to the manager. Try not to be the one to say, "No." Because your income is directly connected to your customer's attitude, you always want to appear to be on your customer's side. Try to let the manager be the one who has to say, "Sorry. Can't do it. Company policy."

While these steps will work for most customers, there are some tough characters who require special treatment:

"Hostile Harry"

You can tell from the way he starts in on you as you approach the table or how he snaps at you when you ask him a question that "Hostile Harry" is one snarling dog.

Remember that 99% of the time his lousy attitude and rude behavior have absolutely nothing to do with you! He was like this when he came in.

Even though listening to this guy may be the last thing you want to do, it is the key to successfully handling him. Get him talking about his favorite subject, himself, and he will lay off you.

Harry: "Seems like I've been sitting here for an hour! Where the hell have you been?"

You: "It sounds like you have had a tough day. What happened?"

Harry: "This pie is awful."

You: "Some of our other customers were also surprised that blackberry doesn't taste anything like blueberry. It sounds like you have had some other surprises today. What happened?"

"Skeptical Susan"

Probably a cousin to "Hostile Harry", "Skeptical Susan" expects the worst. She's the type who looks for bones in a tuna fish sandwich. You'll know it's "Susan" by her cynical and sarcastic tone. You will never win an argument with this one so don't even try.

A better strategy is to let her say her piece and respond in a way that shows her you respect her question and are on her side. Underneath her aggression, she desperately wants to be right and taken seriously. Give her what she wants.

Susan: "If I order the burger will it come out raw and bloody like last time?"

You: "You are absolutely right. That's important to know. How would you like your burger prepared?"

"Know-it-all Ned"

This guy is out to impress: you, those dining with him, everyone in the restaurant if he can. Let him. Give this guy opportunities to show-off and he will reward you for it. The "alternate close" and the "add-on close" will work well but watch the time. "Know-it-all Ned" will just keep talking if you don't control the situation.

You: "Sir do think a first class Chardonnay or a Chenin Blanc would be a better choice for your and the lady's meal?"

Ned: "Why of course the Chardonnay for both. It would enhance all the subtle flavors in the sauce for the fish. The buttery flavor of the Chardonnay would highlight the ...."

You: (interrupting him) "Absolutely sir. I will bring you a two glasses of our finest Chardonnay immediately."

"Superstar Sam"

This high-profile character goes to great trouble to be noticed. He will do almost anything to feel important. As with "Ned," flattery works well here. Compliment his choices and use the "add-on close" to give him opportunities to be a hero.

> You: "Excellent choice sir. Two orders of Prime Rib. Medium for you, rare for the lady. Unless I miss my guess, you're the type who appreciates something special. We have a rather special wine that I am sure would delight you and your guest. Shall I bring the bottle?"

"Indecisive Irma"

She seems sweet but she can really cause trouble. Her inability to reach a decision and to stick with it when she finally does reach one can screw up the timing for all of your other tables. Handle "Irma" with a warm but firm touch. Give her "either/or" choices and a lot of reassurance that she is safe with her decisions. The three F's (feel, felt, found) work very well for this type. Be sure you end the exchange with a question that forces her to choose.

> (After the third time you have stopped by her table to see if she was ready to order)

> Irma: "I am not very hungry today so I am not sure what I want."

> You: "I understand how you feel. A lot of my customers have felt the same way. They found that either the chef salad or the soup and sandwich special was just perfect. Which one sounds better to you?"

Even after "Irma" has made a decision and placed her order, this one can still cause problems.

(As you return to her table to deliver her lunch)

Irma: "I'm not sure I want the tuna salad. I think I would like to change my order."

You: "I understand how you feel. I've felt the same way - that what I ordered might not be what I really wanted. I have found that once I start eating, I realized I had made just the right choice. I am sure you did too."

"Hurry-up Hank"

With all this guy says he has to do, it's amazing that he is even taking time to eat. You will earn points with this type if you acknowledge his being in a rush and cut out all chit-chat. You will lose points if you lecture him on why slowing down is better for his health or by trying to sell him anything once he has asked for the check

Errors and the time "wasted" correcting them make this type very upset so be sure you understand everything about his order. You can use "Hank's" need for speed by suggesting he "complete" his order:

Hank: "I want the chicken parm, Italian dressing on the salad and coffee black."

You: "I can hear that you are in a rush. So there is no delay, would you like to place your dessert order now?"

Aggravation Saver

The customer may always be "right"
but there is a difference between "Server" and "Servant."
You do not have to sacrifice self-respect for a tip.

Stress Relief

Rule # 1: Don't sweat the small stuff.
Rule # 2: It's all small stuff.

Dr. Christian Bernard

Veteran servers suggest that the single best way to avoid "Burn out" is to accept that no waiter or waitress can be perfect in every customer's eyes. To paraphrase Lincoln, "You can please some of the people all of the time and all of the people some of the time, but you can't please all of the people all of the time."

Smarter servers strive for personal excellence not perfection. They accept that occasionally they might forget to put the dressing on the side or even drop a plate.

Whether you plan to stay in the restaurant industry for a month, a year, or a decade, realistic expectations are essential to your mental, physical, and emotional health. But until we all become enlightened Buddhas, here are three techniques that offer immediate mental and physical relief from the stress and tension of restaurant life.

Eyestrain Reducer

This exercise remedy takes two minutes and is great for relieving strained, tired eyes.

Start by washing and drying your hands. Place your thumbs along your nose and gently slide your thumbs across the upper rim of both eye sockets, moving from your nose out toward your temples. Use your finger tips to massage the lower rims of your eye sockets, also working from your nose out to the temples. Do the tops and bottoms of your eyes three times. Now with your eyes closed, slowly look for side to side three times, up and down three times, and finally in three complete circles. Take three full deep breaths and open your eyes.

Imaging

This is a wonderfully refreshing way to take a mental holiday. Start by finding a place where you can safely shut your eyes for three minutes. Take a few deep breaths as you let your mind wander off to a pleasant place. You might take a mental walk along a cool forest path, or curl up in an abandoned lifeguard stand at the edge of a deserted beach, or raise a glass of lemonade in a flower filled meadow. Whatever your destination, move into your image with all of your senses.

Imagine the crunch of leaves under your feet as you walk through the forest. Smell the salt spray of the gently rolling waves. Hear the wind in the grass and the song of the birds in the meadow.

Enjoy a few more deep breaths as you feel the energy of Mother Earth revitalizing you before you slowly open your eyes and return to present time.

Alternate Nostril Breathing

This technique sounded more than a little weird when servers in Southern California first described it; but after a group of waitresses in Iowa also suggested it, I gave it a try and felt it deserved inclusion. Try it for yourself. You will find that this yoga breathing technique actually seems to balance your brain.

Start by washing and drying your hands and then finding a place where you can relax for three minutes. It does not matter whether you sit or stand but find a position that fully supports your body. Rest the index and middle fingers of one hand on the space between your eyebrows. Observe your breath. Notice which nostril is flowing more freely. This is the "active" nostril. The other we will refer to as the "passive" nostril.

Depending on which finger is more appropriate, use either your index or middle finger to gently press the "active" nostril closed. Inhale and exhale slowly and fully through the "passive" nostril. Release the pressure on the "active" nostril. Gently use a finger to close the "passive" nostril and take a full deep breath through the "active" nostril. Switch back and close the "active" nostril. Inhale and exhale. Switch and close the "passive" nostril. Inhale and exhale.

After five or six breaths per side, allow both nostrils to remain open as you take three finishing breaths. Notice how clear and focused your thinking has become.

Of course, you will feel less stressed and be able to perform at a higher level if you take good care of yourself outside the restaurant. You will enjoy your time as a server and be more successful (make more money!) if you provide sufficient energy to your mind and body. Fuel your body with the right mix of food, sleep, oxygen, and exercise.

Unfortunately most people do not do even what they know is best for themselves. Every body benefits from eating small, healthy meals. Most people overeat on junk. Get eight to ten hours of sleep? The American Medical Association says sleep depravation is an epidemic in this country. The human body needs oxygen. Most people are very shallow breathers. Every body would benefit from 4 half hour aerobic sessions each week, but even though there are 336 half hour units in a week, most people spend only 2 half hour periods doing any kind of aerobic activity.

Food, sleep, oxygen, exercise. There are two more items long-time servers suggest you add to the list.

Shoes. If you work in a restaurant, you need the right shoes. Servers spend all of their work time walking or standing so it is well worth the investment in time and money to find a pair of shoes that fits well, supports and cushions your feet, and has the type of sole that won't slip when the kitchen floor gets a bit messy.

Aggravation Saver

Buy yourself good quality shoes for work!
Your ability to walk without slipping and to work without
pain is directly linked to the quality of your shoes.

Expect to spend approximately $100 per pair.

(Even though that $10 pair at the discount store
looks the same, they are not the same.)

If you are working full time, get a massage once a month. After a busy shift your shoulders and back will ache and your legs will feel like you've walked miles. Even your face will feel tense (from masking your emotions). Whether you choose Swedish, Shiatsu, or some other style, a massage once a month is more valuable and less expensive than you think.

Aggravation Saver

Servers all across America voted,

"One hour under the skilled hands
of a massage therapist"

as the #1 stress reliever.

Food, sleep, oxygen, exercise, good shoes, and a massage once a month. Find the right balance and you will become sharper, better able to use all you've learned to provide superior service and earn great tips.